UN
STOP
PABLE

Published by N. Cindy Trimm, LLC
Stockbridge, GA

For information on other resources or to place an order, please contact:

Trimm International, Inc.
950 Eagles Landing Parkway #347
Stockbridge, GA 30281
Tel: 678-565-9888

Website: www.trimminternational.com
Email: info@trimminternational.com
Facebook: www.facebook.com/drtrimm
Twitter: www.twitter.com/cindytrimm
LinkedIn: www.linkedin.com/in/drtrimm

Trimm, Dr. N. Cindy
Unstoppable: Compete with Your Best Self and Win
ISBN: 978-1-931635-09-7
Library of Congress Control Number: 2021917614

Printed in the United States of America

UN STOP PABLE

COMPETE
WITH YOUR BEST SELF &
WIN!

CINDY TRIMM

Dare to imagine what life could look like if you took the limits off...

CINDY TRIMM
PRESENTS

UNSTOPPABLE
unstoppablemasterclass.com

Contents

FOREWORD

I have had the pleasure of not only knowing and working with Dr. Trimm for over twenty years, but also the honor of being her friend. We have spent countless hours discussing insights on human potential and a shared vision for human development. I consider her an esteemed colleague and collaborator in working to help ordinary individuals live extraordinary lives.

Dr. Trimm is a pioneering thought leader, futurist, life strategist, entrepreneur, and leader of leaders. If anyone is qualified to speak into your life and revolutionize your career, business, or brand, it is Dr. Cindy Trimm. She is truly an unstoppable force in her own right! In this masterpiece you are holding in your hand, you will find all you need to live and lead in the same unstoppable fashion.

When I reflect on my own life and career, I recall that when there were times I felt defeated, gave into doubts, or couldn't seem to find the energy to move forward, life would send me a voice. Someone would come into my life, even if just for a moment, and give me a message that reached into my heart and psyche and encouraged me to take the next step on my path. The right voice at the right time can be the catalyst you need to change your thinking and propel you in the direction of your destiny.

Dr. Cindy Trimm is such a voice.

She is here to tell you that despite world events that seem to threaten our very existence; despite your circumstances, your environment, or your past—or most of all, your self-limiting beliefs—you too can become unstoppable. You've got something special inside of you; you've got greatness within you. You are an unrepeatable miracle put here to achieve incredible goals, live your wildest dreams, and make a positive difference in the world.

So, what is stopping you?

Too many of us live our lives trapped in doubt, fear, and holding on to past events and circumstances that we've allowed to define our current life narrative. This collective tangle of negative thoughts and feelings prohibits us from performing at our best and pursuing our greatness. It breaks my heart to see such potential for greatness wasted. Don't end up in the cemetery with your gifts and genius still buried inside. Become a grave robber!

As you read *Unstoppable*, prepare to be elevated and empowered to unlock the hidden layers of yourself and remove the internal barriers keeping you from the success you desire and the life you deserve. *Unstoppable: Compete with Yourself and Win* will take you to a place within yourself that you've never been before—a place where you will discover your truth and find the courage to live it on your own terms. Each chapter is designed to introduce you to a part of yourself that is waiting for you to push through and tap into the drive and passion needed to live full and die empty.

In *Unstoppable*, Dr. Trimm reveals how often we live as though we are in constant competition with others to achieve success, when in actuality, the only competition that matters is the one with our own selves. She shows that being *Unstoppable* is what will separate you from the distractions, the people, or anything that is not relevant to your own winning future. Being *Unstoppable* will introduce you to the people, energy, and experiences that will allow you to get up again one more time or for the one millionth time when life knocks you down or you are facing challenges.

You deserve what is waiting for you on the other side of the finish line. You deserve to live in the winner's circle! Like Dr. Cindy Trimm, it's your time to be *Unstoppable!* You can trust her to show you how.

That's my story, and I'm sticking to it.

LES BROWN, Speaker, Author, Trainer

INTRODUCTION

"We attain freedom as we let go of whatever does not reflect our magnificence.
A bird cannot fly high or far with a stone tied to its back. But release the impediment,
and we are free to soar to unprecedented heights."

~ALAN COHEN

What are the impediments keeping you from soaring to unprecedented heights? What keeps you from reflecting your magnificence? A simple, unfettered approach to life could be what frees you to achieve greater success and happiness. Without being constantly overwhelmed by trying to force things, life can unfold until it flows as if it were effortless.

Forrest Gump depicts such a life. Forrest, famously played by Tom Hanks, was born with all the odds stacked against him, yet he grew up to be an authentically good-hearted person. Because of his optimism—the lens through which he saw the world—he was able to break social boundaries, unflinchingly step into the center of historical events, and become a true hero. He seemed to be unstoppable. Unlike the characters around him, Forrest was not bound by trying to control how life unfolded. Instead, he made the best of whatever life brought him—and he lived his truth. He intuitively understood that life was not happening to him, but happening for him; and discovered his own potential for greatness as a result.

The message of the movie boils down to this: You may not be blessed with riches, intelligence, prominent family connections, or good looks, but if your heart is in the right place, your impact on this world will be tremendous. Like Forrest Gump, if you dare to show up in life authentically, if you are courageous enough to live your truth, you too can become unstoppable.

Let me ask you: What is that personal truth you've lacked the courage to express? What are the limiting beliefs that hold you back? What is keeping you from moving forward, going further… flying higher, or simply getting ahead? Have you ever wanted to raise the bar of your life—your own personal standards for how you live? Or have you become so accustomed to being "grounded" that you've stopped trying to fly?

Few things are as discouraging as feeling "stuck." If you've ever experienced a stagnant season, or if perhaps you are mired in one now, you know how uninspiring life is without a sense of direction. In those moments, it's common to ask yourself:

Does what I do matter?
Do I matter?
If what I do and who I am matters, to whom does it matter?

Being stuck isn't all bad. It creates the necessary intensity of desire to break free and discover new meaning for living. It heralds a need for change and reveals life strategies that no longer work. You learn what tools in your proverbial shed must be upgraded in order to pry yourself free from a "stuck" state of mind.

It is what brought you here.

I suspect you picked up this book because you want more. Maybe you feel constrained by circumstances that seem beyond your control. Or maybe you just have a desire to make things better. In either case, you know that your life holds greater potential than your current reality suggests. You know, deep within yourself, that you are destined to win—even if you don't know exactly what winning entails or *how* to get on your path to unstoppable success.

Thankfully, "stuck" does not have to be a permanent condition for you or anyone else. As I've often heard it said, "If you don't like how something is, change it!" And I would add, if you don't like the way *you* are, change *you!*

Unstoppable: Compete with Your Best Self and Win is the first book in my self-mastery series. It is an introduction to the model upon which all of my life and leadership programs are built. I call this powerful four-layered framework the Core4 System. First you must master your mindset, then your behaviors, followed by mastering your personal brand, which positions you for leadership mastery. Gaining competency in these four dimensions will positively influence how you show up in the world. It's a transformational process that builds upon itself to help you answer those tough questions about your place and purpose at this time in history.

The process begins with knowing who you are and living from the inside out. Your mindset and the stories you tell yourself are all controllable factors that can either help you soar or keep you grounded. Getting your head and heart right is the crux of winning in the competition with yourself. That's why Section One, "Win from Within," is devoted to helping you discover and define who you are—and more importantly, who you really want to be. We'll uncover your true identity, as well as your core values, and we'll evaluate the way you think about yourself. You'll want to continually remind yourself of the truths you discover, because the battle within is never-ending. Each time you reach a higher level of achievement, new doubts and fears will arise. When that happens, go back to the beginning and remind yourself of what you know to be true and right for you.

To the foundation of self-knowledge, we add *skills for success.* Knowing who you are is essential, but if you don't behave in a manner that is congruent with that truth—pretending to be something or someone you're not—you will constantly feel disconnected, dissatisfied, misunderstood, undervalued, and anxious. In Section Two, "Wired to Win," you'll learn how to be authentic in your everyday interactions. You'll learn practical communication strategies so you can be true to your identity and values while still honoring other people's unique personalities. You'll also learn tactics for breaking bad habits and creating new, winning habits that support your unstoppable, authentic self. And because this section focuses on interpersonal authenticity—being real with and around others—we'll examine what it means to live your truth by living a transparent life.

Success is first an inside job. If you're accustomed to keeping your guard up, you might as well recognize that in today's continually connected world, transparency is the key to establishing strong relationships and a solid reputation. Establishing a foundational set of success skills will prepare you for the next core: *strategies for growth and significance*. This involves networking, building your platform, and establishing your personal brand. Section Three, "Winfluence," acknowledges that you can only go so far alone. Relationships, be they with your family and friends, with co-workers, or with your extended networks, are the way you reach beyond your own life to make a difference in the world. This section looks at the influence you have now, as well as how to increase it by crafting an unstoppable personal brand and cultivating winning credibility.

Finally, we'll combine everything you've learned and apply it in the fourth core, which is all about *leadership*…and building a lasting legacy by serving the greater good. Section Four, "The Winner's Circle," focuses on maximizing your identity, virtues, and relationships to make a positive, lasting impact; leaving a legacy for the next generation of female leaders to emulate.

Today, I want to invite you into my Winner's Circle.

*Join me now for a free bonus training
at www.winnerscircle.online*

You'll learn the difference between perfection and excellence, between a job and work, and between leading and managing, as well as why service is an elemental part of your legacy. And it's here that you'll define your life's purpose—the mark you will leave on the world—not for notoriety's sake, but for the betterment of others. In my mind, fulfilling your life's purpose is the ultimate win because it isn't about you; it's about how you transform and improve those whose lives your life has touched. For me, this is the true meaning of living an unstoppable life.

In my Executive Life Coaching™ practice, as well as in my other mentorship and life empowerment programs, I work with clients to gain mastery in these four areas throughout the course of an entire year. *Unstoppable: Compete with Your Best Self and Win* introduces you to all four components and shows you how they work together to build an unstoppable, winning life. In each subsequent book, we will focus exclusively on one core area so you can accelerate your pace in your race for your own proverbial gold.

It is my hope that this life empowerment model will transform the way you think about yourself and your place in the world. You will be challenged and encouraged to discover exactly how you can experience a bigger, bolder, and more meaningful life. This journey isn't for the faint of heart; it is for those willing to look within, dig deep, and do the work required to discover what it really means to win.

Do you have the courage to transition from a primal state to a powerful state of being?

Are you ready to pivot to the next best version of yourself?

This book, along with my free bonus training, will help you chart your personal path to success. It will equip you with the resolve to pursue your dreams and inspire a personal commitment to make the changes necessary for a winning life. It will equip you to compete by empowering you to free yourself from the limiting beliefs, self-sabotaging habits, and success-undermining behaviors that have been holding you back. You'll learn that to get unstuck—to soar higher and go farther—you must always take the next first step; make that next winning decision. One destiny-defining step at a time is how you build unstoppable momentum. Because the truth is, one decision can shift your course and put you on the path to becoming your own greatest champion.

If you're ready to compete with the next best version of yourself *and win*, take the first step with me now!

SECTION ONE
WIN FROM WITHIN

"Always dream and shoot higher than you know you can do.
Don't bother just to be better than your contemporaries or predecessors.
Try to be better than yourself."

~WILLIAM FAULKNER

When you embark on any great journey, you need a few critical pieces of information: where you are, where you want to go, and how you're going to get there. This first section of *Unstoppable: Compete with Yourself and Win* will help you find your starting point for the amazing, life-transforming journey you're beginning—as well as your destination. We will start with both the beginning *and* the end in mind: Where you are now vis a vis where you want—*really, truly want*—to go. What are your aspirations? Where do you see yourself personally, professionally, relationally, and financially—ten, twenty, and thirty years from now?

What does it mean to win *for you*?

While I can help you in your search for an answer, I can't tell you exactly what winning looks like as it concerns *you*. Winning is personal. It means that you have (or are) accomplishing what you set out to achieve over your lifetime. It means you are evolving as a person and have a clear sense of purpose. Small wins along the way—a promotion at work, a milestone anniversary, the completion of a course, the refinement of a skill, the breaking of a self-sabotaging habit, the exhilarating feeling you get when you know you are doing exactly the right thing at exactly the right time—let you know you're on the right path. In the same way, you know you've taken a wrong turn when you aren't true to yourself, or when you commit to something at cross-purposes with your core values.

In the next few chapters, you'll discover who you are from the inside out so you can better plan your course. I'll help you figure out what drives you. And if something or someone other than you is in the driver's seat, I'll show you how to take control of the wheel by changing the way you think about yourself and your place in this world.

YOU BECOME UNSTOPPABLE ONE DECISION AT A TIME.

Once you've defined your true identity, we'll look at what it means to live with integrity. You'll discover that a winning life is a harmonious life—one in which your mindset and actions affirm who you are. If your behaviors don't support your beliefs and core values, you'll learn how to bring them into alignment.

And as we close this section, we'll look at the immense power you have over the reality you experience. Every choice you make shapes your destiny. You become unstoppable one decision at a time.

Self-knowledge—knowing who you are, what you believe, and what you value—empowers you to intentionally design the most amazing life of your dreams, and to strategize how you will live powerfully, while uncompromisingly authentically. You are about to learn that the only way you can truly win is to be the best, most authentic, unstoppable *YOU* possible!

Chapter 1

WIN AT BEING YOU

*"When you are content to simply be yourself
and don't compare or compete, everybody will respect you."*

-LAO TZU

I was so excited.

It was sports day at my school, and there I was, suited up like every other five-year-old: white sneakers, navy-blue shorts ironed with a crease, my hair combed back in a ponytail, and a clean, crisp white T-shirt. I looked around and didn't feel like the poor kid I had come to identify myself with. That day, I belonged.

They announced the shoelace race and asked us to take off our sneakers and put them on the starting line. As did everyone else, so did I, even though I had no idea what a shoelace race was. Then we walked a few paces away to get ready for the race.

A teacher called out, "On your mark! Get set!" and then, letting the anticipation build in the air, "*Go!*"

Everyone ran to their sneakers and put them on, and then, one by one, started running to the finish line. Everyone except me, that is. I was lost and didn't know what was happening. It was at that moment I realized I didn't have the one essential skill necessary to run that race. I didn't know how to tie my shoes!

As you can imagine, in a busy household with six older siblings, it was always easier for someone to tie my shoes for me than take the time to teach me, so I had never learned. It had never really mattered—until that moment.

I heard my mom call out, "Cindy, just go!"

The kids were saying, "C'mon, Cindy!"

And the teachers were calling out, "Run, run, run!"

But I didn't budge.

In that moment, I realized I was missing a skill. Without this skill, I no longer belonged.

There were several reactions I could have had. I could have cried. I could have run the race without tying my laces as others were urging me to do. I could have gotten mad at my family for never teaching me to tie my own shoes. I could have thrown a fit.

But instead, I made the decision then and there: I was not leaving that line without knowing how to tie my shoelaces!

In the pandemonium, a teacher came to me and started to tie my shoe for me. "No," I told her. "Teach me how! Please?"

She looked at me for a moment, then smiled. It was as if everything around us stopped. The teacher knelt and methodically showed me what to do on one shoe, while I repeated it on the other. The whole school and all the spectators who had come for that sports day waited and watched as I learned to tie my shoelaces through the tears running down my face. I didn't care about the race. I didn't care who was ahead of me. I had just found my own race to run, and for now it was learning to tie my sneakers.

You should have heard the cheers as I stood up and ran for the finish line that day. I finished last, but they gave me a special consolation prize. Maybe the teachers felt sorry for me, or maybe they wanted to reward the determination I'd shown. I don't know. But that was the day I learned that the most important races are always the ones with yourself—they are always the ones that help you grow and improve your chances of winning the next time you race.

That day, learning to tie my shoes was my race, and I needed to compete with myself and no one else. I needed to grow, and I needed to overcome a weakness that was holding me back. So I did, and I gained new clarity about who I was and what I was capable of doing. That has defined all of my races ever since. That was the day I learned to run my own race, compete with the next best version of myself, and always grow better and stronger with each win.

It took an unexpected test to bring out the next best version of myself. I discovered my potential on the fly—a skill that I was unaware of; one that remained dormant in the form of potential until it was summoned. What you don't know about your own hidden abilities, skills, and potential could be hampering your progress, while learning new things about yourself positions you to win your next race. Like my race, it can be something you learn on the fly—there on the starting line of your own personal race to greatness.

> THE MOST IMPORTANT RACES ARE ALWAYS THE ONES WITH YOURSELF.

I would like to add here that there is an overemphasis on putting the best picture of yourself out there for others to see, when you should be focusing on the substance behind those façades. Do you just go with the flow to "save face" as perhaps I could have done—taking the path of least resistance? Or do you expand your capacity to do better—to be better—regardless of how that might look to others. This is where you find your own brand of genius.

You are an original. You have no competition.

On the face of this earth, no one else possesses your unique combination of gifts, skills, and abilities. No one has the exact same education or knowledge as you do, because the way you hear, interpret, and internalize information is unique. No one else has the exact same history or the same dreams for their future. Even identical twins, who share almost the exact same genetic makeup, have different fingerprints, personalities, and experiences. You are one of a kind.

Since no one is exactly like you, your only competition *is you*.

I know. That's not what the world tells you.

The world tells you that if you want to accomplish anything great in life, you've got to compete with others. The unfortunate belief driving this type of competition is that we are all vying for the same scarce resources. Only one winner can prevail. That zero-sum mindset makes everyone an opponent and almost every encounter a win-or-lose situation. The media, your boss, even your family members are happy to remind you that life's stakes are high. One mistake, one wrong word, one less-than-stellar idea, one too many slices of cake can lead to disgrace, a lost sale, a broken relationship, a financial loss, or any number of other disastrous outcomes. And to make matters worse, someone else will gain because of your loss. It's a fatal-flaw theory that drives thoughts of scarcity—that there's only so much (opportunities, jobs, wealth, etc.) to go around.

Author and social researcher Brené Brown notes that this scarcity mindset makes life scary and disheartening. She states, "These are anxious and fearful times, and everywhere we hear the lexicon of scarcity. We are not rich, thin, or beautiful enough; we are not safe, perfect, or powerful enough; and ordinary lives are completely dismissed."[1] It's no wonder, then, that so many people are plagued by self-doubt, insecurity, and a paralyzing fear of failure. Rather than identifying and reaching for their dreams, the tendency is for people to look outside themselves for guidance and fulfillment. They look at others and doubt themselves. Questions and self-defeating thoughts take over: "Should I be doing what so-and-so over there is doing? She looks more successful than I am. I could never be like her. I will never win."

I'm here to tell you that you were born winning.

Your biological beginning is proof that you are a born winner. Out of 250 million "others" competing for gold—the proverbial golden egg—at conception, you won! You were preprogrammed to maximize your potential and utilize your full capacity as a winner. If you could do that without a fully developed mind, or fully developed heart, hands, feet and eyes, can you imagine what you can do, accomplish, and achieve now that you have them? You are unstoppable!

You are one of a kind—an original. That means the only true competition you have is with yourself. And here's some exceptionally great news: In a competition, someone must always be declared the winner. But as Roger Staubach once said, "Winning isn't getting ahead of others. It's getting ahead of yourself." If you compete with yourself…you are guaranteed to win!

Now, you may be thinking, "Cindy Trimm, how do I compete with *myself*?"

We all know how to win a race against other runners. Run faster than everyone else and you win. When competition is based on quantifiable differences that measure the fastest, strongest, smartest, most popular, or bestselling, it is easy to determine the winner. Tally the numbers and award the prize to the person with the highest score.

> THE ONLY TRUE COMPETITION YOU HAVE IS WITH YOURSELF.

But if you're competing against yourself, how do you gauge progress? How do you know if you're winning? It's all about knowing that you have the potential at any given moment to become a better version of yourself.

If you are looking outward, you can't see how much potential you really have.

So, you must look inward.

Judith Orloff, psychiatrist and author of *Emotional Freedom*, wrote, "Your life is explicitly designed for your own growth."[2] She's right. Comparing yourself with others is futile. No matter how good you are in one area, someone will always trump you in another.

It's human nature to measure your prosperity or success against that of your friends, your acquaintances, your co-workers, and society at large. Maybe that's why one of the Ten Commandments is "do not covet" what others have.[3] Comparing yourself to others leads to feelings of inadequacy, dissatisfaction, and worse of all, jealousy—all self-destructive primal states. When I speak of "primal," I am referring to those negative fight-or-flight emotions of fear, doubt, anger, jealousy, insecurity, etc. Most people respond to negative circumstances from a primal emotional state of weakness, rather than from a powerful, elevated state of strength. Every day, you must choose between a primal or a powerful response.

If you're going to compete with yourself and win, you must stop looking for external validation. Others' achievements will never give you an accurate measure of your own inherent potential. Here are a few ways comparisons are unfair, unhelpful, and unhealthy:

- As Albert Einstein is credited to have said: "Everybody is a genius. But if you judge a fish by its ability to climb a tree, it will spend its whole life believing that it is stupid."
- When you compare your beginning with someone else's completion, you fail to factor in the heartache and hard work they put into achieving their goal. Comparisons like this can make you feel defeated before you even start.
- Comparisons leave you with the feeling that you don't measure up. Or...comparisons give you a feeling of superiority. Neither inferiority nor superiority are beneficial states of being.
- Your winning should never be based on another person's success or failure. There will always be someone stronger, faster, smarter, or better looking—none of which has anything to do with YOU winning at being YOU.

The truth is, what others are or are not doing is irrelevant. Your own growth is the fruit of success. When you compete with yourself, you look for positive change, improvement, and personal development over time. This is not an overnight job, but a lifelong quest. You begin to ask questions like, "What can I do today that I couldn't do five years ago, one year ago, six months ago...yesterday?" You recognize that you may not be where you want to end up—emotionally, financially, in your relationships, or with your career—but you are on your way. You are making incremental progress day by day.

When my niece was two years old, I observed her running from one end of the hallway to the other. When she got to the first end, she would throw up her arms and shout, "I weeunnn!" She did this for five straight minutes, until I asked her, "What are you doing." In her Mickey Mouse voice, she said with a glint in her eye, "I *wace* (race) with myself and I *weeunnn* (win)!"

Since you are measuring personal growth against your own personal potential, the first step in this competition with yourself is to tap into that self-belief—to get clear on your personal identity—to understand who you are and what you want. Where are you now versus where you want to go? What is most important to you? And most importantly, how will you become the person, build the career, and create the life you desire?

Viktor E. Frankl wrote in *Man's Search for Meaning*:

> Everyone has his own specific vocation or mission in life; everyone must carry out a concrete assignment that demands fulfillment. Therein he cannot be replaced, nor can his life be repeated, thus, everyone's task is unique to his specific opportunity to implement it.[4]

You have a purpose and a mission that is unique to you. Until you know and acknowledge who you are, it is impossible for you to fulfill your purpose.

For this reason, we will begin this journey by discovering your true identity—the first of the four core pillars in my Core 4

Empowerment Program. The ultimate goal of living what I call an "empowered life" is your ability to fulfill your purpose: your own particular assignment, mission, or "calling," as some describe it.

Every person has that inner longing to know they are here for a reason, that their life has meaning, and that the world will be different because they walked on its stage. In working with people from all walks of life from all over the world, I've discovered that those who struggle most are individuals who are uncertain or unclear about who they are and what their purpose is.

Issues of identity not only damage your psychological health, but also have negative physiological and social effects. When you don't know who you are or how you fit into the world, you will inevitably experience frustration and unease that can present symptoms such as emotional distress, physical disease, and failed relationships.

I've recently heard it said that what looks like resistance, in all its various forms, is often a lack of clarity. Once you are clear about what makes you tick, what drives you, what you stand for (and what you won't), and what you want to accomplish or achieve in life, you can begin competing for gold—going higher, faster, stronger than you thought possible.

That journey begins with self-knowledge and ends with self-mastery.

WHAT IS YOUR TRUE IDENTITY?

"Who you are, what your values are, what you stand for. . . They are your anchor, your north star. You won't find them in a book. You'll find them in your soul."
-ANNE MULCAHY, FORMER CHAIRMAN AND CEO, XEROX

Who are you?

Do you know?

Without falling back on a title, can you with all certainty tell me, yourself, your friends and family members, your boss, or your employees who you truly are and what you stand for?

Most people can't.

Most people allow others to define them. The vast majority of us define ourselves based on a title or a role. We then waste our precious energy and time trying to live up to others' expectations and demands. Most of us know more about what other people think of us and want from us than we know about our own thoughts and desires; we know more about what people expect of us than what we expect of and desire for ourselves!

But that's not going to be true for you, at least not anymore. If you're ready to commit to this journey of transformation—of personal growth—then you must get honest with yourself and establish (or own up to) your true identity. The only way to truly succeed in life is to live authentically—to appreciate who you are and express yourself honestly to the world. You've already heard me mention that this is an inside job. The last and grandest of our human exploration is not outer space but inner space.

So, who are you?

When I ask audiences this question, I frequently hear statements such as:

> I'm a doctor.
> I'm a lawyer.
> I'm an insurance broker.
> I'm a mother.
> I'm a father.
> I'm an author.
> I'm a salesperson.
> I'm a professor.

None of those titles are bad or wrong, but that's the thing— they are just titles you wear, roles you fill, and in some cases, the masks you hide behind. Your work may help you express your gifts, talents, and abilities, but it doesn't (or at least it shouldn't) define you. If your identity is wrapped around your job, what happens when you get laid off, or when the company folds, or when you retire? If your identity, career, or job title are inextricably linked, then you would be lost in a limbo of inner conflict and confusion.

No, your identity is not determined by your title.

Some people answer the question, "Who are you?" by looking to their family or their personal history. Now, I do believe your heritage (where you come from) and your inheritance (what you were born into) can contribute to what you believe about yourself. But as with your roles, neither should define you. I was born into poverty. If I chose to limit my potential to the kind of lifestyle I inherited at birth, I never would have

THE LAST AND GRANDEST OF HUMAN EXPLORATION IS NOT OUTER SPACE, BUT INNER SPACE.

become the youngest senator appointed in my home country of Bermuda. I wouldn't have become a bestselling author, a successful entrepreneur, a trained psychotherapist, or a public speaker who has inspired audiences around the world.

The same is true for your life. If you allow your heritage or family history to establish the expectations for who you should be, how you should believe, or what you should accomplish (or are capable or incapable of accomplishing), you will never grasp the extent of your potential. Your history is a stepping-stone on the path to your future; you're not meant to set up camp there.

YOUR PAST DOESN'T DEFINE YOU

Another faulty way people tend to define themselves is by their past behaviors, achievements, failures, or circumstances. For example, you might hear someone answer the question, "Who are you?" with statements like:

I'm a hard worker.

I'm an athlete.

I'm an animal lover.

I'm an introvert.

I'm a widow/widower.

I'm an alcoholic.

I'm an activist.

I'm an ex-convict.

I'm a recovering addict.

I'm a single parent.

I'm a cancer survivor.

Even if the statement is true, at best it is a surface-level description of your circumstances or your past. Your past is not your prison, nor is it a predictor of your future. Your past behavior does not define you as an individual. And as with your lineage, when you buy in to those external labels, you limit your potential for becoming anything greater.

So, if other people's expectations, your titles, your history, your past behavior, or your present circumstances don't define you, what does?

You do.

APPRECIATE WHO YOU ARE

So many people believe they have to be something they aren't if they want to succeed.

That lie is a trap that will keep you bound to a life spent struggling in mediocrity.

The truth is, your dreams, passions, desires, and hopes are all seeds of greatness buried deep within you. They exist only because you *already possess* the potential for achieving them!

Does that mean you can just sit back and allow the sun and rain to do the work so you can reap a harvest?

Of course not.

You already have the creativity and the ability to succeed. However, success—whatever you determine that means for you—will require you to work the soil of your heart, to nourish it with positive and value-adding information, and to weed out negative attitudes, bad habits, and disempowering beliefs.

You don't have to become something you're not in order to succeed. You have to become more of who you are.

INTENTIONALLY CRAFTING YOUR IDENTITY

One of life's great joys is that you have the ability and freedom to be the person you want to be. In fact, you are the only one with the right to determine your identity. Your identity is not fixed and static. It is dynamic. Every day and every stage of your life you will discover more about the depth and breadth of who you are.

Your indisputable authority over your identity gives you the power to create your future. Your identity—what you believe about yourself—shapes the narrative of your story. In any given moment, you get to determine the plot twists. What you've overcome to accomplish your goals and achieve your dreams, whom you are able to help, the success you enjoy in business, your financial wealth, and the richness of the relationships you have with others are all influenced by the identity you create.

That should be excellent news!

Do you feel excited? Energized? Enthusiastic about your future?

Not yet? Well, our journey is just beginning.

I've actually had people tell me they were astounded to learn that not only do they possess the ability, but they have the *responsibility* to determine their identity, to refine their temperament, and to polish their personality. They were, perhaps like you, dissatisfied with their stories and personal life narratives. They didn't like their career, they had outgrown a relationship or were unhappy with their financial situation, or they were lonely. Life wasn't going as planned.

That's when I ask: "Could things be the way they are because you are the way you are?"

The answer, of course, is a resounding "Yes."

It's convenient to abdicate one's responsibility. It's easier to hold someone else liable for your challenges and difficult situations; to believe that if only the market was better, or your boss was kinder, or if other people weren't so annoying . . . then you could have the life you really wanted.

Rather than be discouraged or overwhelmed, I hope you will choose to be empowered by the news that you have the ability to change your circumstances and results. You are not a prisoner of your past or present. The moment you make the decision to change, you can change your reality. If you want to have more, you must first become more. You must look within. The first and best place to look to create real and lasting change is within yourself.

> COULD THINGS BE THE WAY THEY ARE BECAUSE YOU ARE THE WAY YOU ARE?

Your identity is shaped by your *beliefs* about your ability, personal power, talents, and potential. You can become the person you want to be by *choosing* what to believe about yourself and your capabilities. In the words of Viktor Frankl, "Everything can be taken from a man but one thing: the last of human freedoms—to choose one's attitude in any given set of circumstances, to choose one's own way."[5]

You must be intentional about crafting your identity. Otherwise, you will be relegated to a mediocre life in which others decide who you are and how far you can go. Don't allow that to happen, because mediocrity is a place where your dreams and potential go to die! I promise, there is more in you and to you than what other people can imagine for you.

EVALUATE YOUR MINDSET

How you see yourself influences how you behave, which influences how you grow, which influences how you interact with others and impact the world. Your beliefs are shaped by your thoughts and words. They are perpetuated by your actions. And they become your future. If you want to change your life—to craft an identity that reveals a capable, successful, strong, and respected individual—you must begin to see yourself that way. Your mind will accept whatever you tell it to believe. If you tell yourself you are strong, smart, and capable, your mind will believe it and act accordingly.

Unfortunately, most people give their minds a far less encouraging script to follow.

The Law of Cause and Effect states that good causes bring good effects, and bad causes bring bad effects. Likewise, your own cause (thoughts/deeds) brings about your own effect. There is always an inner cause for every outer effect. That's true for your circumstances, and it's true for your identity. If you don't want to see something in your future, don't think about it today. What occupies your mind today will eventually fill your mouth, and the words you speak eventually become your reality. James Allen said:

> The outer conditions of a person's life will always be found to be harmoniously related to his inner state. This does not mean that a man's circumstances at any given time are an indication of his entire character, but that these circumstances are so intimately connected with some vital thought-element within himself that, for the time being, they are indispensable to his development.[6]

Everything you are, experience, and ultimately achieve can be traced back to how you use your thoughts and words. The most empowering part of this truth is that if you do not like where you are or who you are, you are only one thought from turning toward the life you desire and becoming the person you want to be—one action away from changing how you feel. According to Gretchen Rubin, author of the *New York Times* bestseller *The Happiness Project*, you can change the way you think simply by changing how you act. It begins by being intentional about your thoughts and actions. You must think and act the way you want to feel.

CHANGE YOUR THINKING, CHANGE YOUR LIFE

Most of our thoughts (and actions) are habitual, meaning that we don't consciously think about or choose them. They pop in and out of our minds based on what we've heard from the world around us and what we've told ourselves before. In *Happy for No Reason*, Marci Shimoff writes:

> According to scientists, we have about 60,000 thoughts a day. That's one thought per second during every waking hour. No wonder we're so tired at the end of the day! And what's even more startling is that of those 60,000 thoughts, 95 percent are the same thoughts you had yesterday, and the day before, and the day before that.[7]

It's like putting your entire life on stutter. No wonder we are unsuccessful in breaking unwanted cycles of sadness, failure, and stagnation. Rarely do we actually think about thinking. The norm is to sit back and let our minds run as they wish. But thoughts are—or at least they should be—a choice rather than a habit. While the right physical habits can help you achieve amazing things, habitually negative thoughts can keep you stuck in a rut. I challenge you to consciously and daily conduct a thought audit.

Because the mind is continually in search of growth, it tends to spray thoughts like Silly String—chasing down rabbit trails. Our minds are insatiably curious. This is why we habitually scroll through Instagram feeds or click random YouTube videos. Instead of thoughtlessly letting our minds wander, we should be challenging our minds to learn new things. As the first-century Christian writer the apostle Paul explained, you are "transformed by the renewing of your mind,"[8] not by sitting back and thinking the same old thoughts.

Hara Estroff Marano, editor of *Psychology Today*, wrote in an article titled "Depression Doing the Thinking":

> Thoughts are mistakenly seen as privileged, occupying a rarefied territory, immune to being affected by mood and feelings, and therefore representing some immutable truth.
>
> Compounding the matter is that negative thinking slips into the brain under the radar of conscious awareness and becomes one of the strongest of habit patterns. People generate negative thoughts so automatically they are unaware that it is happening, that it is actually a choice they are making.[9]

If you want to change your life and intentionally shape your identity, you can begin today by changing your thinking. That starts by paying attention to the thoughts you allow to race through your mind and weeding out those that are keeping you from living authentically. Here's an activity that will help you recognize disempowering thoughts and replace them with words that reflect the truth and reality you want to experience.

Step 1. Audit Your Thoughts

Keep a thought journal. Use a small notebook to record the thoughts that pass through your mind. Do this for several days and then look back and see which words and phrases are most frequently repeated. Mark all the negative, self-defeating, discouraging, or fearful thoughts that are cluttering your mind.

Step 2. Put Your Thoughts to the Truth Test

Look at the negative thoughts you've marked and ask yourself, "Is this statement 100 percent true?" You may have written down statements such as, "I'm always late," or even, "I'm so stupid." If you're honest with yourself, you will realize that those thoughts are not true. More than likely, you were embarrassed or angry or fearful in that moment and your mind took the opportunity to criticize rather than encourage you.

Step 3. Displace Negative Thoughts with Positive Thoughts

Telling someone to stop thinking a certain way will not reverse negative thinking. Negative thinking must be displaced with positive thinking. Norman Vincent Peale noted that, "Displacement is the only way you can drive a thought from the mind."

For every negative thought you've recorded, write down an opposite, positive thought to displace those negative words. For example, if your thought was, "I'm always late," your new belief

> *TAKING CONTROL OF YOUR THOUGHT LIFE IS CRUCIAL TO BECOMING UNSTOPPABLE.*

might be, "I'm getting better at managing my use of time." If your thought was, "I'm so stupid," demand that your brain treats you better by writing down something like, "I'm intelligent and creative. My worth doesn't come from perfection."

Taking control of your thought life is crucial to becoming unstoppable. As Earl Nightingale, author of *The Strangest Secret*, said, "Whatever we plant in our subconscious mind and nourish with repetition and emotion will one day become a reality."

REWRITE YOUR STORY

Earlier in this chapter, I mentioned that people often allow their past to define their future. The tendency is to retell our stories until they become the soundtracks that drive our present reality—like the musical score of a film pushes its scenes along.

Change your narrative about your life. Insist on a plot twist. Refuse to see yourself as a victim of circumstances. Ultimately, you don't attract what you want, you attract to yourself what you believe about who you are. You must therefore remove your self-imposed limitations.

All professional therapy and personal counseling are built upon this one fundamental principle—that there is a boundless, infinite, and limitless potential within every human being to surmount any condition, experience, or situation once self-imposed limitations are removed.

CHANGE WHAT YOU BELIEVE ABOUT YOURSELF TO BE TRUE.

When you change what you believe about yourself to be true—change that internal script—your story can become a personal source of inspiration when days get hard, because it will remind you of how far you've come. It can motivate you to keep pressing forward. And it can encourage and embolden others.

I've also discovered, however, that retelling our stories can hurt us if we aren't careful. Telling your truth is not the same thing as telling your story. For example, my own story starts like this:

Some people are born with silver spoons, others with plastic. I was born with no spoon. When I was two years old, my father left my mother with seven children. We ended up living in poverty...in a run-down home where the roof leaked, rats scuttled across the floor, and sometimes we didn't have water to drink.

(Can you hear the melancholy music playing behind the words?)

No one would have blamed me for continuing to live in poverty after such a hard childhood. I could have retold my story for sympathy a thousand times, and people would have held my hand and cried with me over the unfairness of life every time. I could have perpetuated the story until my children were telling it to their grandchildren as their own.

My story may have had a sorrowful beginning, but that's not how I chose to finish it. I insisted on a plot twist. I proudly tell people that my story isn't sad, because what my mother gave me is a sense of self-worth, dignity, and significance greater than the weight of all the gold you could offer me. She taught me faith—she taught me how to believe in God and in myself. I don't remember a day when my mother told us we didn't have "enough." She taught all of my siblings how to honor the wisdom spoken from elders. She showed us how to save, how to show respect, and how to be nonjudgmental. She insisted, "If you don't have money or things to give back to society and your community, give service." She demonstrated the value of an honest day's work, excellence, and ethics. Her example and the life lessons she engrained in my siblings and me are the driving force that keep us all stable and centered today. When I think about the strength I gained from my childhood, I get excited! The empowering lessons I learned and gladly share from my story center around the theme that no hardship, challenge, or circumstance is insurmountable.

We all get hurt and have sad stories. Life gives us all the proverbial rope-a-dope experiences. But I've learned that when you tell your story for pity, you sink deeper into the problem. In contrast, when you tell your story to extrapolate principles that offer life lessons, you grow and progress. The hard times and difficulties we endure can reveal secrets to our prosperity and success. What principles have you learned from your life experiences?

Each time you tell your story, you become more like the person in the story. That's why you must choose to tell your story for principles—for the lessons you've learned from your experiences. I learned many lessons that took the struggle out of my stride. I learned that I was not only the CEO of me, I was the creator of my destiny and reality. Don't play the supporting actor when you've been cast in the leading role. Refuse to play the antagonist in the unfolding of your life story when you've been cast to play the protagonist. Allow positive words to swell with a triumphant crescendo that pushes you toward a life of success!

Take a few moments to think about the stories you tell about your life. When you share them, what do you hope to gain? What emotions do you want the other person to experience? If you are hoping (even secretly) for sympathy, *stop*. You may be in collusion with your pain, suffering, betrayal, abandonment, abuse, or disappointment. You may be looking for a psychological coconspirator with your imposter syndrome. Your life does not have to be like this anymore. From now on, I want to encourage you to see yourself differently. No one can go back to an old beginning to change anything. But you can start right now by making a simple adjustment to create a new and powerful ending. Don't tell your story again until you can turn it into one that empowers you and others. Yes, talk about the pain, but also talk about your defining moment— the painful moment that pointed you to purpose—the one that summoned your potential. Otherwise, you risk being dragged into a self-sabotaging pit of defeatism—living from a primal state of self-imposed limitation. Instead, think about what lessons you've learned from your experiences. How have you grown as a result? What will you do differently going forward?

Look for the principles in your story that reveal your strength of character and your true identity. Tell your truth—talk about your dreams, abilities, gifts, and awesome personality. Look in the mirror often, because the person staring back at you is the real hero or shero you've been looking for. That person has the responsibility of helping you out of your "stuck" state.

THE WINNER IN YOU

If you want to get to know someone extraordinary and powerful, get to know yourself. It's all about self-knowledge. You can start by solidifying in your mind who you are. Get to know your true identity.

Our present idea of *identity* is a fairly recent and complex social and psychological construct. Even though it is used in everyday conversation, it is challenging to provide an adequate definition that captures the depth and range of its meaning.

Your identity is amazingly complex with hundreds of intertwining facets and characteristics. Your identity encapsulates everything you were, are, and have the potential to become. Your identity is molecular energy in motion. Think "I-dent-it." Your identity is your expression of self that influences other people's perception of that expression. It is the X-factor of your personal brand. Your identity is the collective aspect of a set of facets by which you are definitively recognizable or known separate and apart from someone else, and involves both your genotype and phenotype. Much like your genetic code—the instructions in a gene that tell a specific cell how to make a specific protein—your "identity code" is generated in similar fashion at the moment of conception. Like a computer program, or perhaps a better metaphor would be an algorithm, your identity provides a complete set of well-defined bio-chemical instructions of how you, as a human being, are designed to function; how you are wired to live, think, perceive, and operate.

When you are able to live according to who you truly are, you put yourself in the driver's seat of your life. You are able to own your story and speak your truth. When you crack your identity code, you will not only discover your truth, but you will be given the tools and fuel to live life more aligned with the best version of yourself. You will not only evolve as a stronger, more courageous and confident individual who is able to surmount anything, you will rid yourself of the pervasive imposter syndrome.

We all love larger-than-life individuals—and that individual can be you. When you cast aside your self-imposed limitations, insecurities, and fears, you become larger. You become larger in personal power, larger in authenticity, larger in significance, larger in influence, and larger in terms of making this world a better place. You will no longer feel like you have to shrink in the presence of people you perceive larger than yourself, because you will know that their largeness does not diminish your greatness. You will be able to live life with purpose, follow your passion, pursue the right fields of study, hone your skills and abilities, progress and succeed in quantum fashion just by being and believing in yourself.

I cannot guarantee that you will live longer or wealthier—that is all based on your personal habits—but I can guarantee you will live a better, richer, more dynamic, fulfilling, and meaningful life; one that is filled with greater peace, joy, sense of accomplishment, significance, purpose, and wellbeing. Unlimited possibilities will be the hallmark of your daily existence.

I call this living inside out.

Living inside out allows you to live authentically according to who you are genetically programmed to be. Your identity is amazing. Don't let negative thoughts about yourself distort it. It's magnificent. So, display it with complete abandon with all the contours of its beauty, brilliance, and radiance. When you do, this world will at once become a more beautiful and better world to live in.

WINNING ACTION: *DEFINE YOUR IDENTITY*

In this chapter we've looked at what your identity is and what it isn't. Remember that you are the only one with the authority to decide who you are. Carefully choose the words, thoughts, and stories you will use to describe yourself. They will become your reality!

My challenge to you is to write at least five "I-Statements" in your journal that describe the person you are (or desire to become). I've included a list of attributes below, but please, do not limit yourself to these words. You know best who you are and who you are becoming.

Awesome

Brilliant

Comfortable in my own skin

Confident

Courageous

Creative

Decisive

Dependable

Designed to...

Detailed

Discerning

Encouraging

Energetic

Engaging

Faithful

Friendly

Fulfilling my purpose to...

Funny

Generous

Good

Growing

Happy

Helping people to....

Honest

Hopeful

Intelligent

Joyful

Kind

Likable

Loving

On a mission to...

Optimistic

Organized

Patient

Peaceful

Persistent

Powerful

Prayerful

Resourceful

Responsible

Smart

Successful

Talented

Trustworthy

Warm

Chapter 2

WIN AT INTEGRITY

"To be nobody but yourself—in a world which is doing its best, night and day,
to make you everybody else—means to fight the hardest battle
which any human being can fight; and to never stop fighting."

-E.E. CUMMINGS, *A POET'S ADVICE*

I hope you took some time to work through the Winning Action at the close of the previous chapter, because until you know yourself, it's impossible to *be yourself.* Which is why in this chapter, we will explore what it means to live authentically and with *integrity.*

Integrity is a powerful word with a twofold meaning. The first, and perhaps most common usage of the word has to do with honesty. The phrase "a person of integrity" brings to mind words such as *trustworthy, credible, ethical, honorable,* and *unshakable in one's beliefs.* We want people of integrity in positions of leadership because we trust that they will be true to their values and their words. We'll discuss the importance of being a person of integrity as it relates to your relationship with others and reputation in Section Three. Before we get there, I want to talk about how integrity relates to the relationship you have with yourself—*living authentically*—and why you can't truly win in life without it.

WHAT DOES IT MEAN TO LIVE WITH INTEGRITY?

The aspect of integrity that we'll focus on in this chapter concerns wholeness, cohesion, and unity. *Merriam-Webster* offers this as one of the definitions of integrity: "The quality or state of being *complete* or *undivided.*" Can you say that about your life right now?

YOU ARE COMPLETE, EVEN IF YOU AREN'T "FINISHED"

Just as the world tells us we must compete against others to win, a constant message filters through the media, through advertising, in our workplaces, even from our friends and family members, telling us we are not *enough.* Think about the advertising that invades our lives daily. Companies spend millions to convince you that if you buy the car, the suit or dress, the shoes, the diamonds, the house, the all-inclusive vacation package, the newest smartphone or techno-gadget, *then* your life will be complete. But you had better hurry. Quantities are limited.

I HAVE ENOUGH. I AM ENOUGH.

That's the scarcity mentality surfacing again. It's the lie that stuff equals success, and there's only so much stuff to go around. But as Brené Brown reminds us, "Success and high achievement will not gratify us when our self-worth is tied to the mindset of scarcity. We think the opposite of scarcity is abundance—more time, more money—when really the opposite of scarcity is 'enough.' Just enough."[10]

So, I'm here to save you some money. Put your credit cards away. Take a deep breath, and tell yourself, "I have *enough.* I am *enough.*"

Once there was an emperor in the Far East who was growing old and knew it was coming time to choose his successor. Instead of choosing one of his assistants or one of his own children, he decided to do something different. He called all the young people in the kingdom together one day. He said, "It has come time for me to step down and to choose the next emperor. I have decided to choose one of you." The kids were shocked! But the emperor continued. "I am going to give each one of you a seed today. One seed. It is a very special seed. I want you to go home, plant the seed, water it and come back here one year from today with what you have grown from this one seed. I will then judge the plants that you bring to me, and the one I choose will be the next emperor of the kingdom!"

There was one boy named Ling who was there that day and he, like the others, received a seed. He went home and excitedly told his mother the whole story. She helped him get a pot and some planting soil, and he planted the seed and watered it carefully. Every day he would water it and watch to see if it had grown. After about three weeks, some of the other youths began to talk about their seeds and the plants that were beginning to grow. Ling kept going home and checking his seed, but nothing ever grew. Three weeks, four weeks, five weeks went by. Still nothing. By now others were talking about their plants but Ling didn't have a plant, and he felt like a failure. Six months went by, still nothing in Ling's pot. He just knew he had killed his seed. Everyone else had trees and tall plants, but he had nothing. Ling didn't say anything to his friends, however. He just kept waiting for his seed to grow. A year finally went by, and all the youths of the kingdom brought their plants to the emperor for inspection. Ling told his mother that he wasn't going to take an empty pot. But she encouraged him to go, and to take his pot, and to be honest about what happened. Ling felt sick to his stomach, but he knew his mother was right. So he took his empty pot to the palace.

When Ling arrived, he was amazed at the variety of plants grown by all the other youths. They were beautiful, in all shapes and sizes. Ling put his empty pot on the floor and many of the other kids laughed at him. A few felt sorry for him and just said, "Hey nice try." When the emperor arrived, he surveyed the room and greeted the young people. Ling just tried to hide in the back. "My, what great plants, trees and flowers you have grown," said the emperor. "Today, one of you will be appointed the next emperor!" All of a sudden, the emperor spotted Ling at the back of the room with his empty pot. He ordered his guards to bring him to the front. Ling was terrified. "The emperor knows I'm a failure! Maybe he will have me killed!" When Ling got to the front, the emperor asked his name. "My name is Ling," he replied. All the kids were laughing and making fun of him. The emperor asked everyone to quiet down. He looked at Ling, and then announced to the crowd, "Behold your new emperor! His name is Ling!" Ling couldn't believe it. Ling couldn't even grow his seed. How could he be the new emperor? Then the emperor said, "One year ago today, I gave everyone here a seed. I told you to take the seed, plant it, water it, and bring it back to me today. But I gave you all boiled seeds which would not grow. All of you, except Ling, have brought me trees and plants and flowers. When you found that the seed would not grow, you substituted another seed for the one I gave you. Ling was the only one with the integrity, courage and honesty to bring me a pot with my seed in it. Therefore, he is the one who will be the new emperor!"[11]

My mother quipped in broken-record fashion, "Cindy, it's the little things that count." Integrity—wholeness of character, with no area tainted by the compromising of core values—does not come from and is not proven by possessions or "once in a lifetime" experiences. You cannot take shortcuts in life and arrive at integrity. It comes from knowing and simply *being* true to who you are when no one is watching. It is comprised of those core values and characteristics that are forged in the crucible of challenging, difficult, and disappointing life experiences. It is not only about the lessons you learn but about who you become once you emerge from them. This is what makes you a wonderful expression of truth and a force to be reckoned with.

Here's the truth: If you look to something outside yourself to complete you, you will live in continual risk of incompleteness. That which is outside of you can be stolen or damaged. Marriages fall apart. People pass away. Markets fail. "New and improved" technologies come along and make your expensive toys and tools obsolete, putting you back into a state of lack.

Your experiences, no matter how hard or difficult, are mirrors that reflect who you really are at your core. Growing up, a teacher shared this poem with me by an unknown author:

> *I asked for strength and God gave me difficulties to make me strong.*
> *I asked for wisdom and God gave me problems to solve.*
> *I asked for prosperity and God gave me brawn and brain to work.*
> *I asked for courage and God gave me dangers to overcome.*
> *I asked for patience and God placed me in situations*
> *   where I was forced to wait.*
> *I asked for love and God gave me troubled people to help.*
> *I asked for favors and God gave me opportunities.*
> *I received nothing I wanted, I received everything I needed.*
> *My prayer has been answered.*

Helen Keller beautifully sums up the crux of this poem with one statement: "Character cannot be developed in ease and quiet; only through experiences of trial and suffering can the soul be strengthened, vision cleared, ambition inspired, and success achieved."

Problems are like a GPS that show us where we are and how we have been living, relative to where we want to be and how we envision living at some distant point in the future. This process helps us to better focus on identifying our core values and to move forward with greater fidelity. Character building starts in the cradle and ends in the grave. Oscar Wilde once said, "Every little action of the common day makes or unmakes character, and that therefore what one has done in the secret chamber, one has someday to cry aloud from the housetop."[12]

PROBLEMS ARE LIKE A GPS THAT SHOW US WHERE WE ARE AND HOW WE HAVE BEEN LIVING.

Those character-building moments morph into capacity-building moments that make you the person you are. The key to you becoming unstoppable is to keep growing—to keep challenging yourself to dig deeper within your mental, emotional, and spiritual reservoirs for whatever you need to face the challenges before you. You will not fully know what you are made of until opposition comes, and you hoist the sails of your values and principles and navigate through opposing forces. Only then will you arrive at your own happy haven of true peace, success, and prosperity.

Character and integrity are about wholeness. Wholeness gives you a sense of *enoughness*—that state of being complete.

Now, does being complete mean that you've finished growing? Of course not! We all have continual opportunities for growth. Remember: Growth is the fruit of your success. Tying apples to a tree doesn't make the tree productive or fruitful. Only the tree that produces its own fruit is seen as healthy and successful. In the same way, you will never experience completeness by acquiring material possessions and/or developing even the best relationships. Your success comes from within. Your "fruit" is made visible when you live with integrity and express your authentic self by sharing your virtues, values, beliefs, and abilities.

You are already complete. That's the truth.

Now you must make the choice to both own and live that truth.

UNDIVIDED: STANDING STRONG

Abraham Lincoln quoted from my favorite book when he shared the truth that "a house divided against itself cannot stand."[13] When two entities stand in strong opposition to one another, it is challenging—and very often impossible—to exist harmoniously in the same space. One keeps pushing against the other until the structure collapses in a heap, broken and burned by an ensuing explosion of emotions.

The same is true for your life. When you say one thing but do another, you lack integrity.

Integrity is not about untruths told to others, but it is the lies you tell yourself about yourself.

We all know how this looks in a public forum. It's the political leader who makes promises on the campaign trail but fails to deliver once they are in office. Or a corporate executive who "guarantees" success even though she knows the product or service is flawed. But what about the personal promises you make to yourself, perhaps promises no one knows about? What about all the goals you've set and excuses you've made for not reaching them? Have you sworn off sugar only to continually indulge in sweet treats and sugary drinks…or promised yourself you'd be in bed by 10:00 p.m., only to stay up surfing the net or binge-watching your favorite show? What about the promise you made to walk ten thousand steps a day, but never averaging more than two thousand because you are "so busy"?

I can hear you now exclaiming, "Oh no, not me!" You may very well be the type of person who would never lie or cheat others, but I wonder if you are committing those offenses against yourself. For example:

- Do you honestly believe that exercise and healthy eating habits are essential to your physical well-being, but you consistently overindulge at the dinner table and never make it to the gym?
- Do you claim that your children and spouse are the most important people in your life, but you spend more time with your co-workers and clients than with your family?

- Do you value financial independence but continue to use credit cards and accumulate debt?
- Do you, deep down, have a desire to do something great, but hold back because you wonder what others will think?

If your values are at odds with your actions, your house—your sense of self—is divided and at risk of collapsing.

Living an integrated, authentic life is a choice that must be acted upon daily. In his book *Today Matters*, John Maxwell wrote, "Successful people make the right decisions early and then manage those decisions daily." If you want to win, you must first decide what's important to you and then commit to putting those priorities first. Then, *every day*, you must choose to be intentional about staying true to your decisions so that your values match your actions. That's how you live undivided. Decide who you are, what you value, and then, as Shakespeare said, "To thine own self be true."

LIVING AN INTEGRATED, AUTHENTIC LIFE IS A CHOICE THAT MUST BE ACTED UPON DAILY.

What does that look like in real life?

If you value your health, take care of it daily by making smart food choices and exercising regularly.

If you value your spouse and children, make them a priority on your schedule. If you tell your child you will be at his or her school performance, be there. If you promise your spouse you will spend time together on the weekend, don't bring work home with you on Friday afternoon.

If you value financial independence, learn how to live within your means and save a portion of your earnings each month. Better yet, find ways to create additional income.

If you value your dreams, refuse to let others' opinions, doubts, fears, or failures stop you from pursuing them!

Is it easy?

No.

Is it worth it?

Well, let's see. People who live inauthentic lives tend to:

- Spend money on things they don't need (or want) simply because they desire to impress others.
- Waste precious time doing things they don't like because they feel compelled to (you guessed it) live up to other people's expectations.
- Deny their dreams and purpose so they can "fit in."

On the other hand, those who live authentic lives invest their time with the people most dear to them. They use their valuable resources to work on goals that are important to *them*. Most importantly, when they look back on the sum of their life, they are at peace, knowing they wouldn't change a single thing.

Does that sound worth it to you?

STAND UP, STAND OUT

Sometimes the challenge of living authentically isn't a question of knowing what you want. It's a fear that if people knew who and how you really are, they wouldn't like or accept you. Psychologists call this "imposter syndrome."

So, we soften the edges. Tone it down. Pull it back. We don't embrace all that we are or could be because people might think we're weird, too intense, too passionate, or too "out there." We either fall into the trap of feeling like we're faking it, or the habit of dumbing ourselves down so as not to make waves.

Let's look at what living a less-than-authentic life has gotten us so far:

A world of minimal differentiation. Walk through any mega store in the United States and you'll see all sorts of "choices" of products that are basically the same. Suburban neighborhoods are lined with houses that all look alike. Same. Same. Same. Sounds pretty boring, doesn't it? In Chapter 9, we will take a look at what differentiation means to your personal brand (the way people see and remember you), but for now, it's enough to know that blending in never makes you memorable.

BLENDING IN NEVER MAKES YOU MEMORABLE.

A life of mediocrity. When you settle for an inauthentic life, you end up giving less than your best. After all, why would you bother to push yourself when all you have to do is meet the world's minimum standards? But let me tell you: Living a mediocre life doesn't serve anyone, least of all you. In fact, living below your potential will cause stress and dissatisfaction, and it can lead to feelings of emptiness and depression. I know you want better than that for your life, because you've committed to reading this book.

The need to belong is pervasive in almost every culture worldwide. And yet those who stand up and stand out are known as the heroes, the role models, the success stories.

In what area(s) of your life are you simply maintaining the status quo? What would happen if you decided to give that area of your life your very best effort?

How would maximizing your potential change your life, alter the trajectory of your career, benefit your relationships, improve your health, and increase your happiness?

ARE YOU LIVING AUTHENTICALLY?

What does it mean to live authentically, or to live an authentic life? Does it mean chucking all societal norms for the sake of being different? Or disparaging anything that hints of conformity? Or completely rejecting your culture?

I suppose it can and does mean all those things to some people. In truth, however, your environment and culture have helped you become the person you are today. And in some ways those external forces have probably helped you better define who you want to be going forward. We are not products of nature *or* nurture—but of both. Each person has an individual soul and a core set of values that are unique. And at the same time, no person can totally separate him- or herself from their surroundings and upbringing. One's life experiences can and should serve as lessons and resources from which the future can be shaped if not envisioned. So, I'm going to encourage you to take the best from your culture, your childhood, your career, and your relationships, indeed from all your experiences, and use that information to guide you as you define what your authentic life should look like.

Before we go any further, let's take a closer look at the word *authentic*.

The *Online Etymology Dictionary* offers this description:

"Authoritative," from Old French *autentique* (13c., Modern French *authentique*) "authentic; canonical," and directly from Medieval Latin *authenticus*, from Greek *authentikos*, "original, genuine, principal," from *authentes*, "one acting on one's own authority," from *autos* "self" + *hentes* "doer, being," from PIE **sene-* "to accomplish, achieve." Sense of "entitled to acceptance as factual" is first recorded mid-14c.[14]

Merriam-Webster adds the following to the definition of authenticity:

- Genuine or real; not copied or false
- True and accurate
- True to one's own personality, conscience, or character [15]

GET TO THE CORE

In 1948, psychologist Bertram R. Forer gave a personality test to a group of students and then presented them with what was purported to be a detailed evaluation of their personality based on their results. The students were then asked to rate the accuracy of the description on a scale of 0 to 5; 0 = very poor and 5 = excellent. The students gave an average accuracy rating of an impressive 4.26. Here is the description every student received:

> You have a strong need for other people to like you and for them to admire you. You have a tendency to be critical of yourself. You have a great deal of unused energy which you have not turned to your advantage. While you have some personality weaknesses, you are generally able to compensate for them. Disciplined and controlled on the outside, you tend to be worrisome and insecure inside. At times you have serious doubts as to whether you have made the right decision or done the right thing. You prefer a certain amount of change and variety and become dissatisfied when hemmed in by restrictions and limitations. You pride yourself on being an independent thinker and do not accept other opinions without satisfactory proof. You have found it unwise to be too frank in revealing yourself to others. At times you are extroverted, affable, and sociable, while at other times you are introverted, wary, and reserved. Some of your aspirations tend to be unrealistic.[16]

The lesson is clear. Just because what people say about you seems accurate, valid, and applicable to your life and personality, does not mean that it is. Spend time investigating your own unique genius. I encourage you to take a deep dive. And be careful of sweeping generalizations that probably apply to almost everybody. When you are living authentically, you are acting on your own authority in a manner that is true to your own personality, spirit, or character. Knowing who you are is an essential step toward living a genuine and abundant life.

Knowing what you value is also critically important. *SUCCESS* magazine publisher Darren Hardy explains in his book, *The Compound Effect* (Vanguard Press), that clearly identifying your core values—the aspects of life that drive your thoughts, beliefs, and ultimately your behavior—is what makes it possible to live an authentic life.

> Your core values are your internal compass, your guiding beacon, your personal GPS. They act as the filter through which you run all of life's demands, requests, and temptations, making sure they're leading you toward your intended destination. Getting your core values defined and properly calibrated is one of the most important steps in redirecting your life toward your grandest vision.[17]

DEFINE YOUR CORE VALUES, REDEFINE SUCCESS

When life is extremely busy or stressful, it's easy for our priorities to get out of whack. As Stephen Covey described in *The 7 Habits of Highly Effective People*, we focus on the urgent rather than the important because, let's face it, the squeaky wheel gets the grease. When those important things—our core values and true priorities—go neglected for too long, life crashes in on us. That's what happened to Arianna Huffington in 2007 when she abruptly came to the realization that despite all appearances, she wasn't living a truly successful life. "On the morning of April 6, 2007, I was lying on the floor of my home office in a pool of blood. On my way down, my head had hit the corner of my desk, cutting my eye and breaking my cheekbone," she writes in her book, *Thrive*. Long hours and sheer exhaustion had taken its toll on Huffington. She'd been named one of *Time* magazine's 100 Most Influential People and her two-year-old blog, *The Huffington Post*, was well on its way to becoming one of the most widely read and referenced online news sites. "But after my fall, I had to ask myself, 'Was this what success looks like? Was this the life I wanted?'"[18] Eighteen-hour, high-stress days yielded impressive money and power, but at what cost?

Huffington began a process of identifying what she really valued. Using that self-knowledge, she redefined success. She'd experienced the fame and fortune, and discovered that those highly coveted rewards weren't enough to sustain a healthy and truly meaningful life. Her fall sparked a turning point that led her to create what she calls the "Third Metric"—a more comprehensive way to measure success than relying solely on the markers of money and power. This third metric gives equal weight to intangible yet incredibly important and often undervalued aspects of success: well-being (physical and mental health), wonder (taking delight in the world), wisdom (learning and growing), and giving (sharing one's life with others). These four elements have become integral to the way she measures success. When those priorities take center stage in her life, she knows she is winning.

Your values can and should act as both a compass to direct your path as well as a standard against which to measure your progress. They are not a luxury; they are a necessity for an integrated, authentic life. You've heard the phrase: "If you don't know what you stand for, you'll fall for anything." Defining your core values helps you decide what you will allow in your life, what you will stand for and against. Your values play a vital role in your personal success, and as Richard Barrett states in his book, *The Values-Driven Organization* (2013), they are equally essential for your professional success. "If you want to succeed in business in the era we are now entering, your values must be evidenced in every decision you make and every action you take," Barrett writes. "Furthermore, your behaviors must align with your values—you must be seen to be walking the talk and operating with integrity."[19]

Walking the talk—that is the difference between authenticity and false fronts, between an integrated life and one that's fractured and compartmentalized. Your core values can only empower you if you live them day in and day out. This is what living your truth is all about. And I'm going to tell you right now, living with your values as your practiced priorities can be challenging. Ariana Huffington says that even though she now knows her core values and how they support her definition of true success, it's easy to slip into old habits of overscheduling life and "miss the real point of our lives even as we're living them."[20] She's right. No matter who you are or how much you've accomplished, authenticity—which requires living true to your core values—is a constant choice that requires courage and practice. It takes work, but isn't it empowering to know you have that choice?

> **YOUR CORE VALUES CAN ONLY EMPOWER YOU IF YOU LIVE THEM DAY IN AND DAY OUT.**

Yes, living with your core values as your guide and gold standard will take focus and energy. And there will be times when you will fall short of your best intentions—even if you are fully committed to living an authentic, integrated life. You wouldn't be human otherwise. When those inevitable scenarios occur, pick yourself up, admit the mistake, ask for forgiveness (from others and/or yourself), and move forward. Then, the next time you're faced with a decision, ask yourself, "Does this activity/thought/choice align with my core values?" If so, wonderful! Press on! However, if the activity or its outcome does not reflect your most important values and lead you closer to the life you desire, politely refuse. Remember, each authentic choice you make aligns you with a life that is fully integrated: complete, whole, and undivided.

WINNING ACTION: *WHAT DO YOU VALUE?*

1. Your core values are the principles and standards by which you operate. I call them "non-negotiables." They are the character traits or qualities you want to express through your words and actions.
2. Review the words listed here and circle the ones that resonate with you.
3. Of those you circled, put a star by the ten that best describe the person you want to become and list them in order of importance to you.

Going forward, consider your top ten values to determine how to best use your time, money, energy, and other resources. A good question to gauge the integrity of any activity is: "Would this support my core values?"

Knowing your core values puts you on the path to winning at being the next best version of your unstoppable self.

CORE VALUES

Ability	Affluence	Balance
Abundance	Ambition	Beauty
Acceptance	Approachability	Belongingness
Accomplishment	Assertiveness	Benevolence
Acknowledgment	Assurance	Boldness
Adaptability	Attentiveness	Bravery
Adequacy	Attractiveness	Calmness
Adventure	Availability	Camaraderie
Affection	Awareness	Candor

Capability	Correctness	Encouragement
Carefulness	Courage	Endurance
Certainty	Courtesy	Energy
Challenge	Creativity	Enjoyment
Charity	Credibility	Enlightenment
Charm	Curiosity	Entertainment
Chastity	Daring	Enthusiasm
Cheerfulness	Decisiveness	Exactness
Clarity	Dependability	Excellence
Classy	Depth	Excitement
Cleanliness	Determination	Experience
Cleverness	Devotion	Expertise
Closeness	Dignity	Exploration
Comfort	Diligence	Expressiveness
Commitment	Diplomacy	Extravagance
Compassion	Direction	Facilitating
Competence	Directness	Fairness
Completion	Discernment	Faith
Concentration	Discipline	Fame
Confidence	Discovery	Fascination
Congruency	Discretion	Fashion
Connection	Diversity	Fidelity
Consistency	Duty	Fitness
Contentment	Education	Flexibility
Contribution	Effectiveness	Focus
Control	Efficiency	Fortitude
Conviction	Elegance	Frankness
Cooperation	Empathy	Freedom

Friendliness	Independence	Moderation
Frugality	Industry	Modesty
Fun	Ingenuity	Motivation
Generosity	Inquisitiveness	Neatness
Gentility	Insightfulness	Obedience
Genuineness	Inspiration	Open-mindedness
Giving	Instinctiveness	Openness
Grace	Integrity	Optimism
Gratitude	Intelligence	Organization
Gregariousness	Intensity	Originality
Growth	Intimacy	Passion
Guidance	Intuition	Patience
Happiness	Intuitiveness	Peacefulness
Harmony	Inventiveness	Perceptiveness
Health	Joy	Perfection
Heart	Justice	Perseverance
Helpfulness	Kindness	Persistence
Heroism	Knowledge	Philanthropy
Holiness	Leadership	Playfulness
Honesty	Learning	Pleasantness
Honor	Logic	Pleasure
Hopefulness	Longevity	Poise
Hospitality	Love	Popularity
Humility	Loyalty	Practicality
Humor	Mastery	Precision
Imagination	Maturity	Preparedness
Impact	Meekness	Presence
Impartiality	Mindfulness	Privacy

Professionalism	Self-reliance	Tactfulness
Prosperity	Sensitivity	Teamwork
Prudence	Sensuality	Thankfulness
Punctuality	Serenity	Thoroughness
Purity	Service	Thoughtfulness
Qualification	Sharing	Tidiness
Quickness	Significance	Timeliness
Quietness	Silence	Tradition
Readiness	Simplicity	Tranquility
Realism	Sincerity	Trust
Reason	Skillfulness	Truth
Recognition	Solitude	Understanding
Recreation	Sophistication	Uniqueness
Refinement	Speed	Unity
Reflection	Spirituality	Usefulness
Relaxation	Spontaneity	Variety
Reliability	Stability	Victory
Resilience	Stillness	Virtue
Resolution	Strength	Vision
Resourcefulness	Structure	Vitality
Respect	Success	Warmth
Rest	Sufficiency	Wealth
Restraint	Superbness	Willingness
Sacrifice	Support	Winning
Satisfaction	Supremacy	Wisdom
Security	Surprise	Wonder
Self-control	Sympathy	Worthiness
Selflessness	Synergy	Zeal

Chapter 3

WIN NOW!

"You may not control all the events that happen to you,
but you can decide not to be reduced by them."

-MAYA ANGELOU, *LETTER TO MY DAUGHTER*

How often have you heard someone shout, "Why me?!"

Have you ever been that someone? Have you ever been so challenged and frustrated by life's recurring, perhaps seemingly constant struggles, that your only response to the unfairness of it all is to throw your hands up and demand to know "*why?!*"?

I actually believe "why me?" is a great question. Too often, however, it is used as a complaint or a cry of despair, rather than as the powerful self-discovery tool it could be.

What if, instead of a question of defeat, we used this powerful three-letter word—*why?*—to discover the real problem? What if you asked, "Could things be the way they are because I am the way I am?"

Before we close out this section of the book, I challenge you to honestly evaluate the "Why?" Now, let me warn you, this may not be pleasant. In fact, it may initially hurt or feel scary. But if you address the real problem, you can find a solution.

There are some ground rules that you'll have to follow if you want to get the most out of this exercise:

Rule No. 1: No Blame-Shifting. In *The Success Principles,* Jack Canfield and Janet Switzer make the assertion that your choices have led to your current circumstances. As unpleasant as it sounds, that means you have chosen to be in your current situation. To change your life, you must change your choices. Blaming *someone* (your parents, your boss, the high school counselor who told you that you'd never amount to much) or *something* (the economy, the weather, the current political climate) will never solve your problem.

BECOME THE LEADING ACTOR IN THE UNFOLDING STORY OF YOUR LIFE.

In fact, blaming others makes you powerless. So, no blame-shifting.

Rule No. 2: Take 100 Percent Ownership of the Problem and the Solution. Become the leading actor in the unfolding story of your life. Step front and center stage. Decide right now that you will own—take complete responsibility for—any problem you're facing and its solution. You get to decide on the plot twists, and no one else! Canfield and Switzer write:

> If you want to create the life of your dreams, then you are going to have to take 100% responsibility. That means giving up all your excuses, all your victim stories, all the reasons why you 'can't' and why you 'haven't' up until now, and all your blaming of outside circumstances. You have to give them all up forever.[21]

Even if you sincerely feel that you haven't chosen your circumstances—you can make the choice to deal with them from a place of power, simply by taking ownership of the solution.

So, remember, not only are you *not* going to blame someone or something else, you are going to proactively *take* responsibility for finding and acting on the solution. Deal? Good!

Take a "me moment," get your journal out, and write down your most honest answers to the following questions. Keep asking "why?" until you get to the root of the problem.

Why aren't you where you want to be?

Why did you give up your power?

Why do you consider yourself a statistic?

Why do you keep making poor choices when you know what the right choice is?

Why have you bought in to the lie that this is "as good as it gets"?

Now...what choices are you going to make going forward in order to improve your life?

EVERY CHOICE COUNTS

> "The battle is all over except the 'shouting' when one knows what is wanted
> and has made up his mind to get it, whatever the price may be."
>
> -NAPOLEON HILL

Everyone—even the most successful person you know—wants something more, better, or different for their lives. The difference between those who grab on to the hope of possibility and use it to propel them and those who can't seem to get beyond the "same ol', same ol'," is not financial status or even intelligence. No, the difference between those who win and those who whine is nothing more than mindset. Winning is as simple, and as challenging, as changing your mind. On a daily basis, you must choose between two very different psychological realities—powerless or powerful.

Now, with all the discussion in the previous chapter about being true to yourself and living authentically, it may seem strange now to hear me say that in order to live a better, stronger life, you must now *change* the way you think. You must think for a change! So often, though, the challenges we face and the obstacles that keep us from growing into all that we were created to become, are not external barriers. They are barriers we have created in our own minds. When we change our minds and break down mental barriers, we become unstoppable.

To be clear, I am *not* asking you to change your core values or your identity. Nor am I asking you to change your personality. I said earlier that I believe we are all uniquely designed—no two people are exactly alike. Trying to force yourself to become something or someone you're not is not only futile, but

WHEN WE CHANGE OUR MINDS AND BREAK DOWN MENTAL BARRIERS, WE BECOME UNSTOPPABLE.

also exhausting. Why wear yourself out attempting the impossible, especially when the world needs the unique gifts only you can give? Even if you succeed in transforming the way other people perceive you, if you are not true to your identity, your personality, and your core values, you will *always* feel that something (namely, *you*) is missing from your life.

What I do want you to change is the way you think about yourself, particularly those aspects of yourself that you view negatively. Emotional baggage—feelings of stress, inadequacy, low self-esteem, depression, anxiety, worry, anger, fear, insecurity, judgment—will weigh you down and keep you from going as far as you'd like. Those feelings, which are all very real, are also very often a choice. Get rid of your own self-authored limiting beliefs about who you are and what you're capable of—don't trespass on your own potential!

Earlier, I touched on the fact that when we repeat our stories, they become bigger and more powerful in our lives. Lisa Wimberger, author of *New Beliefs, New Brain*, explains that neuroplasticity—the mind's ability to hold on to, let go of, and/or rewrite stories—is an innate gift. If you're like most people, you continually and unintentionally use that ability to reinforce the things you *don't* like about yourself. Every time you tell yourself that you are not good enough, you strengthen that belief. Eventually, your actions, mood, and speech follow suit, and you begin behaving as if you aren't good enough.

What if, instead, you choose to use the gift of neuroplasticity to your benefit? Rather than remaining on autopilot (which won't get you where you want to go in life), you can form new, positive mental patterns that will, in turn, change your actions, mood, and speech for the better.

If you want to experience something better or more, you must be willing to change your mind. Regardless of your past, you can begin to win now—right now!

Everything you experienced in your life started in your mind. Your current life realities began as thoughts in your own mind. Yet, in spite of everything you have been through, you are here because you "made up your mind" not to quit or to lose. You are closer to winning—experiencing an authentic, happy, hopeful, successful life—than you may have ever imagined. In fact, the very moment you realize it is *possible* for you to overcome the obstacles that have blocked your path up to this point, you will begin to see an improvement in your life. But you must believe and act as if *every* day and *every* choice counts! The truth is, you are always just one decision away from living the life of your dreams.

WHAT ARE YOU WILLING TO FIGHT FOR?

"You may have to fight a battle more than once to win it."

-MARGARET THATCHER

Lisa Wimberger opens *New Beliefs, New Brain* with this thought: "Our lifespan is merely a blip on a screen of vast earth and space history. We have a choice in how we want to spend that precious time. Some of us yield to pain, punishment, stress, and anxiety; others fight hard to choose joy, love, and compassion. Yes, *sometimes we must fight our own selves to access joy.*"[22]

> YOU DON'T GET WHAT YOU WANT IN LIFE; YOU GET WHAT YOU FIGHT FOR.

It is my belief that you don't get what you want in life; you get what you fight for. When you are against the ropes, you must fight back. You must change your "why me?" to "try me!" Decide that your success, your marriage, your children, your future, your happiness, and your health are worth fighting for. Living authentically can be a battle. But if you choose to stand up against the external and internal pressures that threaten to pillage and plunder your true self, you can emerge stronger, more resilient, and better equipped for the next battle.

This fight is about taking control of your own mind and choosing what you will believe, how you think, and how you will respond when faced with difficult or unexpected circumstances. You don't have to take up arms, but I do want to equip you with a few battle strategies so you can intentionally rewrite your stories and toss out the baggage that keeps you from excelling.

Say "I feel" rather than "I am"

When you are waist-deep in a stressful situation, one of the best things you can do is acknowledge your emotions. I'm sure you are aware of the "fight or flight" response, the body and brain's automatic response to stress or trauma. Whether you're a police officer facing down an armed criminal or an executive who just got a call about a delay that is threating to interrupt a critical delivery doesn't matter. To your brain, stress is stress. When you feel threatened (regardless of the trigger or the severity of the potential outcome), your limbic brain's automatic response is to protect you by throwing you into fight-or-flight mode. A surge of chemicals, including adrenaline and cortisol, rushes through your body, allowing you to respond quickly to danger. If you are actually experiencing a life-threatening situation, your primal fight-or-flight response can save you.

For most of us, however, truly dangerous situations are rare. Since the limbic brain doesn't distinguish between real physical threats and everyday stress, it's constantly flipping the "on" switch—sending in waves of adrenaline and cortisol when you don't really need them. The frantic pace of our lives sabotages our bodies so that the automatic, lifesaving response ends up doing more harm than good. According to the Mayo Clinic:

> The long-term activation of the stress-response system—and the subsequent overexposure to cortisol and other stress hormones—can disrupt almost all your body's processes. This puts you at an increased risk of numerous health problems, including anxiety, depression, digestive problems, heart disease, sleep problems, weight gain, memory and concentration impairment. That's why it's so important to learn healthy ways to cope with the stressors in your life.[23]

Shifting your mental activity from the limbic brain (also known as the primitive brain), where your body and thoughts react automatically, to the prefrontal cortex—the part of your brain where activities such as reason and logical thinking occur—allows you to manage stress more effectively. One way to make that shift from reactionary thinking to intentional thinking is to simply admit what you are feeling, or as Dr. Daniel Siegel explains in his book, *Mindsight: The New Science of Personal Transformation*, to "name and tame" the emotions you are experiencing. You can't (and shouldn't) deny emotions. Remember, the goal is to live authentically and transparently, not to wear an "I'm fine" mask while you're still seething underneath. So, go ahead and acknowledge what you feel. Own it, but don't become it. Refuse to let those emotions control you.

"NAME AND TAME" THE EMOTIONS YOU ARE EXPERIENCING.

The next time you feel anger, or fear, or stress welling up, choose to take control of your mindset; rationally address and deal with emotions, because those feelings are indicators of your truth—your core values. This can be as simple as taking a few, long, deep breaths and changing your internal dialogue from "I am" to "I feel." "Consider the difference between saying 'I am sad' and 'I feel sad,'" writes Siegel. "Similar as those two statements may seem, there is actually a profound difference between them. 'I am sad' is a kind of self-definition, and a very limiting one. 'I feel sad' suggests the ability to recognize and acknowledge a feeling, without being consumed by it."[24]

Research shows that when you speak the words "I am," as in "I am so angry," "I am not enough," or "I am afraid," or even, "I am stressed out," you remain in that state for a prolonged period. In other words, as long as you continue to say, "I am angry," you will feel and act angry. It becomes almost impossible to calm down. Saying "I feel…" hands the control over to the rational part of your brain, where you can think about how to deal with your "feelings."

Saying "I feel" rather than "I am" is a simple technique that has an immediate effect on your brain's physical function, lessening the impact of the fight-or-flight response. And because the brain has the ability to learn new patterns of thought and behavior, if you practice this technique regularly, it will (eventually) become a habitual way of processing emotions. "By developing the ability to focus our attention on our internal world, we are picking up a 'scalpel' we can use to re-sculpt our neural pathways, stimulating the growth of areas of the brain that are crucial to mental health,"[25] Siegel explains. Recognizing your feelings for what they are—sensations that may or may not be an accurate measure of the situation you're facing—allows you to question them and, if necessary, change them. (Revisit the exercises in "Change Your Thinking, Change Your Life" on page 32 often in order to displace negative and inaccurate feelings and thoughts with a positive, solution-focused response.)

It may seem simplistic, but this small, conscious battle for your beliefs and mindset can have a cumulative effect. Over time, your immediate response to stressors will be intentional and rational, or emanating from your powerful state, rather than reactionary, or emanating from a primal state. Imagine how empowered you will feel when you have control over this part of your life. It will be easier to:

- Confront difficult situations
- Have positive, productive exchanges in your conversations, rather than arguing with your spouse or children
- Deal with fears and baggage that weigh you down

Start using this battle strategy today and experience the difference it can make in your life!

Take a "Me Moment"

No matter how successful you are in life, success doesn't give you immunity from being human. We all have days when we don't want to get out of bed, when we are compassion-fatigued, or when we are just burned out. But what happens when this feeling lasts for days or weeks or months? What happens when you feel like you've lost your purpose, when you don't know what to do next, or when giving up seems like the best option—whether it's giving up on a diet, a career, a business venture, or a marriage? Over the course of my career, I've had many such moments. But I have also found that when I take me-moments and privately rehearse to myself my "why," it places a defibrillator on my passion and commitment and gets me going again. I am able to find my center. As Simon Sinek says, it all starts with *why*—why you started or engaged in something in the first place. What's your why?

Maybe you can't remember the last time you were happy. Perhaps your big, colorful vision board has slowly drained its color and turned into an uninspiring black-and-white *blaaaah*. Get back that clarity of focus and passion! Here's what I want you to do. Every ninety days, take an entire day or weekend to revisit your big "why" to ensure you're on track and achieving what you envisioned for your life.

As you adjust your mindset and refocus your vision, remember that feeling uncomfortable is part of the journey. Don't be afraid of the emotional hurdles and psychological brick walls that may seem to keep you from moving forward. Randy Pausch, author of *The Last Lecture*, with only a few months to live, said, "The brick walls are there for a reason. The brick walls are not there to keep us out. The brick walls are there to give us a chance to show how badly we want something. Because the brick walls are there to stop the people who don't want it badly enough. They're there to stop the other people."[26]

Lean in. Taking those me-moments allows you to exhale, breathe in the air of fresh perspective, reset, rejuvenate, and refocus. A well-spent me-moment has the power to reinvigorate and enable you to move forward in a manner you might not have thought possible. Sometimes catching your second wind will help you achieve your win. This is what me-moments are all about.

Make yourself a priority. It's important to take time regularly to find your center—to remember who you are and what is important to you. Take time alone to meditate, pray, plan, recharge, and just think. Quiet your mind so you can hear what your soul is wanting to say.

QUIET YOUR MIND SO YOU CAN HEAR WHAT YOUR SOUL IS WANTING TO SAY.

The trouble is, most people try to take me-moments with other people. It's not "we" moments, but "me" moments. How many times have you asked a friend or a colleague for advice rather than sorting through tough issues on your own or looking inward for answers? Your friend has her own issues and doesn't even know where she's going. She can't really help you, but you can bet that she'll offer up some suggestions on how you should get where you want to go. And why not? It's easier to brainstorm solutions to someone else's problems than deal with your own.

Let me tell you something: If people don't know where they are going in life, they're not in a position to show you the way.

So, the first thing to remember about a me-moment is that it should be spent in *solitude*. Just as no one else has the authority to determine your identity, no one else can determine the path you should take to becoming your best self. You will get much further, faster, if you rely not on what others tell you, but upon your own insights, self-knowledge, inspiration, and instinct. When you are alone, you can think your own thoughts without input from other people, the television, Internet, radio, or any other external source.

Not everyone likes to hear that me-moments must be taken alone. Some people equate solitude with loneliness. Others are afraid of what they might learn about themselves when all of the world's distractions are removed. But if you can find the courage to spend some quiet time alone, I promise that even brief times of solitude will strengthen you.

Keep it simple.

Set aside an hour a day, a day a week, a weekend a month, or a week every quarter to spend alone—just you, your thoughts, and your journal. Make time to think through a difficult situation, to create plans for your future, to reflect on your core values, remember who you are, and refocus on where you want to go. I know you want to be strong and well-equipped to fight for what is important to you. (That's why you're reading this book.) Using these simple strategies will prepare you for the battle before it happens. They will empower you to deal with challenges before they arise.

WINNING ACTION: *WHAT ONE CHANGE WILL YOU MAKE TODAY?*

In this chapter we've discussed the importance of your choices, your thoughts, and your willingness to take 100 percent responsibility for your life. Occasionally, you will be faced with monumental decisions—a marriage proposal, or an opportunity to buy, sell, or start a business, for example. At those times, you, of course, want to carefully weigh your options and make wise choices. But those moments of major decision are few compared to the little choices you must make on a daily basis—the cumulative effect of which can cause major consequences. While those "life-altering" decisions are important, they are no more crucial than the thousands of tiny choices you make each and every day. Tiny choices—those that seem negligible at the time—shape the course of your life. Just as the smallest turn of the rudder changes the direction of a massive ship, even minor adjustments, or micro-shifts, in your daily decisions—all of which happen at the speed of thought—can yield dramatic results.

Here's the question I want you to consider: What one thing can you change that will change everything? What attitude, thought pattern, belief, or behavior—if changed (stopped, improved, or tweaked)— could make your life more fulfilling and rewarding?

Could you, for example, choose to:

- Respond rather than react?
- Hold your tongue instead of speak from anger or frustration?
- Make a shopping list and stick to it?
- Create an action plan for the day and follow it?
- Read or listen to something inspiring?
- Be mindful of what you eat rather than snacking thoughtlessly or going without food all day?

- Establish a daily ritual, such as a morning meditation and/or affirmations?
- Set aside 10 percent of your earnings without fail?
- Make a budget that you don't deviate from?
- Institute a regular date night with you and your significant other?
- Go to bed and get up every day at a set time?

None of these choices seem "major," but each—if practiced consistently—could make a significant impact on the results you achieve.

It's like the age-old idiom: *How do you eat an elephant? One bite at a time!* Every choice, thought, action, and step has the power to lead you closer to the life you desire.

> *EVERY CHOICE, THOUGHT, ACTION, AND STEP HAS THE POWER TO LEAD YOU CLOSER TO THE LIFE YOU DESIRE.*

You may need to make several changes to get to your ultimate destination, but as you'll learn in Chapter 5, habits are more successfully formed one at a time. For now, focus on mastering just one pivotal action in order to make that one powerful change.

The one change I will make that could change everything is...

SECTION TWO
WIRED TO WIN

"You are wired to win. Define your game, embrace the challenge and strive to understand yourself in deeper and more meaningful ways."

-GARY JOHN BISHOP

In the previous section, you looked inward to discover what makes you unique, what your core values are, and how you can tap in to your authentic power by creating a winning mindset. Now we're going to talk about interpersonal authenticity—how to remain true to yourself in every interaction you have with others, both in your personal and professional life.

First, you'll learn how understanding your personality style and unique strengths can enable you to communicate more authentically—while allowing others to be themselves, as well. You'll learn a bit about why you think and behave the way you do. And you'll have the opportunity to begin aligning your values with your virtues so you can live stronger with less stress and frustration.

Then, because behavior drives results, we'll discuss how to intentionally shape habits that support who you want to be. The reality is that knowing and doing are two very different things. That's why Chapter 5 is devoted to helping you learn how to break old behavior patterns that are holding you back and integrate new habits that support your goals.

Once you know how you are uniquely wired and which habits you may want to change or rewire, we'll begin looking at how you present yourself to the world. Authenticity is about knowing and honoring your identity. Transparency is about allowing others to see the real you. How much should you share? What scares you about letting people "look behind the curtain"? In the closing chapter of this section, we'll look at why transparency wins every time.

KNOWING AND DOING ARE TWO VERY DIFFERENT THINGS.

Humans are meant to live in community. How many people you allow in your circle will depend on your personality. The depth and significance of those relationships—be they few or many—will be determined by how you interact with others. Hide your real self, and you're sure to meet with disappointment in the race of life. But if you can find the courage to live authentically *and* transparently, winning is within your grasp.

Chapter 4

WINNING CHARACTER

"The very essence of happiness is honesty, sincerity, and truthfulness."

-ORISON SWETT MARDEN

There is perhaps nothing more frustrating or infuriating than seeing a lie paraded, and worse yet, *accepted* as truth.

On December 11, 2008, the FBI arrested Bernie Madoff for securities fraud. You probably watched as news reports of this incredible Ponzi scheme unfolded in the media. Thousands upon thousands of investors lost an estimated $50 *billion* as a result of Madoff's deception. For almost two decades, Madoff took people's money, promising to invest it for substantial gains. Instead, he pocketed huge sums and used the rest to keep his scam afloat. He sent his clients regular (fake) reports on how their money had fared in the market. Happy with what they saw, many repeatedly invested their money with him and based their financial futures on the lies in those reports.

A few people suspected that Madoff's claims were too good to be true. Harry Markopolos, a certified fraud examiner and chartered financial analyst, didn't simply suspect Madoff's business wasn't aboveboard; he *knew*. In an attempt to stop Madoff's illegal and fraudulent dealings, Markopolos submitted evidence to the Securities and Exchange Commission (SEC) five times between May 2000 and April 2008. In his book, *No One Would Listen*, Markopolos states:

I was a whistleblower taking on one of the most powerful
men on Wall Street, and at some points through the night-
marish journey, I feared for both my safety and that of my
family. I was convinced that the crime he was committing
was going to be the worst in market history. Ten years later,
Madoff is now behind bars and we all know why.[27]

For the better part of a decade, Markopolos watched innocent
people buy in to the lies while regulators repeatedly ignored his
warnings. And when Madoff finally confessed to running the Ponzi
scheme, Markopolos didn't feel vindicated. To the contrary, he told
New York magazine, "I was a $50 billion failure....Why would people
think I feel good about this? People think I'm a hero, but I didn't
stop him. He stopped himself."[28]

Lies can do so much damage that even when the truth is ultimately revealed, we don't feel like celebrating—we feel exhausted,
angry, or both.

"If I take care of my character, my reputation will take care of itself."
-D.L. MOODY

So, what do Madoff and Markopolos have to do with you? Madoff
used his charm and communication skills to take advantage of
others. He promised one thing and did the opposite. Markopolos
experienced intense frustration because he saw a lie perpetuated as
truth. I seriously doubt you're involved in a situation as horrific as
Madoff's scam. But I do wonder if you are in any way attempting to
fool others by pretending to be something you aren't. Now, please
know I'm not accusing you of nefarious or malicious activity. No, the
types of untruths I'm talking about harm *you* more than anyone else.

In the previous three chapters, you invested time in discovering who you are, what really matters to you, and what your core

values are. I hope by now you have a clearer image in mind of the person you want to be. But knowing the truth about yourself and actually *living* from that truth are two very different things. It's easy to put up a front when you're faced with direct opposition or the knowledge (or even suspicion) that by living authentically you face the risk of rejection.

> KNOWLEDGE MUST BECOME ACTION IF YOU ARE GOING TO EXPERIENCE THE WINNING LIFE YOU DESIRE.

This chapter is where the "rubber meets the road," so to speak. This is where knowledge must become action if you are going to experience the winning life you desire.

Very often, people begin self-improvement plans with excellent intentions. They read personal-development books and find the information they need to succeed. From the comfort of their reading chair, they get energized and excited about their potential. Then comes the real-world test, when it's time to put what they know into action.

And as I mentioned in Chapter 2, behaving in a way that is incongruent with your values, beliefs, and identity inevitably results in stress, guilt, frustration, resentment, and even anger. In essence, if you aren't living authentically, you're living a lie. Incongruence between one's deepest desires and behaviors isn't uncommon. Behavior is often a response to our perception of others' expectations. Since you have, I hope, determined to master your mindset and live more authentically, the next step is to set your own expectations for your actions. Set the bar at nothing less than your very best.

COMMUNICATING AUTHENTICALLY IN A COMPLEX WORLD

Understanding how you are wired to interact with others can help you stay true to your authentic self. Recognizing that your "wiring"— your communication style and motivators—is likely different from that of your friends, colleagues, and family members can improve those relationships and help you manage the expectations you have for others. If you are a leader, understanding your own personality and behavioral style, as well as what drives your team members, is especially empowering. It's like having the inside scoop! You'll be able not only to perform better, but also to draw out the best from those around you.

One of the most widely used tools for determining behavioral styles is the DiSC profile. The DiSC profile was originally proposed by William Marston in his 1926 book entitled *Emotions of Normal People.* Since that time, the DiSC profile and assessment tests have been refined and adapted. Today there are several available versions that measure personality and behavior style with surprising accuracy, each describing the four main behavioral types including Dominance, influence, Steadiness, and Conscientiousness.

What the DiSC profile doesn't do is measure intelligence, values, aptitude, or mental health. It is also important to note that no one behavioral style is preferable over another. Every style has its advantages, and *any person* with *any style* can learn to harness his or her strengths to win. So, as we look at the four main personality types in the pages ahead, be honest with yourself about your style and natural tendencies. If you find yourself thinking, *I wish I was like that*, stop and remind yourself that you are uniquely designed and gifted with the attributes that are perfect for you. Determine right now to use your style, whatever it may be, to maximize your own unique potential.*

YOU ARE UNIQUELY DESIGNED AND GIFTED WITH THE ATTRIBUTES THAT ARE PERFECT FOR YOU.

DOMINANT

"What's the bottom line?"

"Get to the point."

"Let's act now!"

---

* Take the DiSC assessment now at www.TrimmInternational.com.

Do these phrases sound like anyone you know? People who are driven to act quickly and decisively have *Dominance* as their primary personality type. This doesn't (necessarily) mean these assertive, determined personality types want to dominate others—but they aren't interested in going with the flow. Their chief goals are personal control and independence.

Competition and challenge motivate high D's (those who measure high on the Dominance scale). When life gets stressful, D's are at their best, ready to take charge, and quick to find the solution that can be implemented *now*. They are self-confident and strong-willed, and they value competence.

As with every personality type, a D's strengths can also be his/her weaknesses:

- A take-charge attitude can seem pushy and overly aggressive.
- A desire to drive ahead may supersede a thorough investigation into better solutions.
- A forceful, strong-willed attitude can be perceived as impatient or insensitive.

If you are a high D, play to your strengths. Just remember that others may need you to slow down. Provide at least a little explanation to your followers so they have the information they need to move forward. Make an effort to be sensitive to others and to listen and consider their input.

If you are not a D personality type, but you are married or a parent to one, or you work closely with someone who is, understand that they have a serious need to be heard. And they *really* don't like being interrupted. Put this person in charge of coming up with the "big picture" plans. With a plan in place, they're happy to delegate the details to others, so they can move on to the next challenge. Also note that a D's greatest fear is being taken advantage of.

INFLUENCER

"Where's the party?"

"Let's get together!"

"When can I come speak to your group?"

Influencers, at their core, are communicators. They are energized by being around people—or rather, when people gather around them. They love being the life of the party. Outgoing, affable, and inspiring, high I's love to talk and make friends easily. They prefer working on a team and are at their best in high-energy environments where change is the norm.

Challenges that high I's need to be aware of include:

- Staying focused. Because I's thrive with variety, keeping on task for long periods of time can feel monotonous.
- Keeping emotions in check. These passionate people tend to feel deeply, show their emotions, and make decisions based on feelings.
- Trying to please everyone. High I's want to make people happy and fear rejection if they don't meet others' expectations.

If you are a high I, use your excellent communication skills to your advantage, but remember to stop and listen to others, too. When you're faced with a big decision, rather than moving too fast, try to step back and consider the pros and cons. Using your heart is good, but being mindful of what's really important to *you* can help you avoid decisions that only please others.

If you are not an I, you may view these enthusiastic, emotional people as flighty or inconsistent. Understand that change is part of their nature. I's can be great team members, especially when guided by clear structures and predefined systems that will help them see a project through to completion. Remember, they aim to please, so correct them gently, and let them know exactly what you need from them.

STEADINESS

"That's the way we've always done it."

"If it isn't broken, don't fix it."

"Why can't we all just get along?"

Those whose personality profile includes a high measure of Steadiness are likely the most loyal people you know. They can be counted on when times are tough. They make both friendships and decisions slowly and carefully. Security is a key motivator for those who score high in S. For that reason, they don't relish change or unrest. They'll go to great lengths to keep the peace.

Challenges faced by these rock-solid individuals include:

- Internalizing negative emotions. These peace-loving individuals avoid confrontation and often bottle up emotions rather than expressing them.
- Being passive-aggressive. They're unlikely to speak their mind if they think doing so will upset others. But that doesn't mean they don't have strong opinions or feelings. If they feel pressured to do something they don't want to do, their response may be one of passive-aggression.
- Thinking the old way is the best or only way. Those high in Steadiness thrive with routine, so change can be difficult.

Steady personality types work well in teams and are excellent when it comes to supporting others. They prefer to let someone else take the spotlight and are happy working behind the scenes. If you're an S, please remember that it is okay for you to express your opinions. You may not feel comfortable doing so as quickly or as loudly as a D or an I personality, but you'll be much happier in the long run if you speak up when you feel strongly about something.

If you are not an S but have the honor of working or living with one, recognize that abrupt changes can be unsettling to these thoughtful individuals. If you know a change is coming, discuss it with them so they have time to adjust. Structure is important to those with an S personality type. Be aware that routines are an essential part of their lives; they aren't trying to confine you so much as they are working to control their environment. If you lead an S, you'll both be happier with their results if you can provide specific instructions, rules, or guidelines.

CONSCIENTIOUS

"What are the rules?"

"I need more information."

"Please don't make me late."

Compliant and *conscientious* are the two words most frequently used as the identifier for the C in DiSC. As each word suggests, rules, structure, and details are important to this personality type. But don't let the word *compliant* fool you into thinking you can push these people around. They are compliant to logic. In fact, they *adore* logic. They use their orderly brains to analyze everything from numbers and news to every aspect of a personal issue. They like neat, well-organized, stable environments. Precise words and clear-cut rules make the C personality types happy—or at least comfortable.

Strong C's may want to watch out for the following:

- A tendency to be harshly self-critical. Self-evaluation is a good thing, but C's have the propensity to take that criticism too far, demanding perfection with little to no room for error.
- Placing more value on facts than people. Because information and details are important to those with a high C personality, they may appear to be calculating rather than caring.
- Being structured to the point of rigidity. C's can seem unwilling to change unless all the facts indicate that change is the absolute right decision. Learning adaptive skills can help C's get along better with others.

If you have strong C characteristics, you probably already know that your analytical abilities are very strong. Use them to your advantage by taking on roles that require fact-finding, and fact-based decision-making. Your calculating style may come off as cold, so keep in mind that just as your feelings run deep and can be easily offended, sensitivity may be the best tool when dealing with others.

If you are not a C but live or work with one, you may find their questions about "how" and "why" tiresome. Rather than trying to push ahead with a C, be patient and willing to supply the facts they need. Doing so will improve your communication as well as your ability to relate to and work well with them. And, please, do not show up late for a meeting with them. Orderliness and promptness are important indicators of quality to C personality types.

BE TRUE TO YOURSELF WITHOUT RUNNING OVER OTHERS

As I mentioned earlier, there are a number of assessments available to help you better understand your personality type, but I bet you can see yourself and your tendencies in at least one of the above four categories. Keep in mind that most people possess qualities from at least two of the personality types. For instance, I am a DI. That means I love a good challenge. I also love talking with people and am energized by helping others succeed. I love creating and establishing new projects, and I hire a team of professionals to manage the details.

When you understand your personality strengths, you can harness them and use them to your advantage. If, on the other hand, you try to behave in ways that are contrary to your natural bent, you'll end up frustrated and exhausted. It's like trying to wear

WHEN YOU UNDERSTAND YOUR PERSONALITY STRENGTHS, YOU CAN HARNESS THEM AND USE THEM TO YOUR ADVANTAGE.

a shoe that doesn't fit. It doesn't matter if the shoe is too narrow, too wide, too short, or too long; if it isn't a perfect fit, it will cause pain, and could even make you stumble and fall.

Let's take this shoe illustration a step further. Imagine that every person in your house, workplace, or community was required to wear the exact same shoe. Why not pick a nice shoe? Let's say a women's size 6, black suede Manolo Blahnik with a four-inch heel. Barney's New York sells them for $595 a pair. Well, the first problem is obvious: Men aren't going to wear such a shoe. And I doubt all the women you know wear a size 6. So, the men, and the women whose feet are too big or too small, are already struggling with the shoe choice they've been forced into. The rest of the women can manage to fit into a size 6, but only a few can walk confidently with that heel height. And of the very small group of women left who are able to stroll gracefully without teetering, not all of them are thrilled with black suede. Some think they are far too expensive and impractical. Others look down at the plain black shoe and wish for a little *bling* or a pop of color.

Harnessing your personality strengths is like finding the perfect shoe—in fit, form, and function. These strengths are your core virtues, and they make you unique and powerful. They color the way you see yourself and the world around you. In the previous section, you identified your core values. I'm willing to wager that if you are living with integrity (whole and undivided), you can see a deep correlation between your virtues and your values. When you are living and communicating authentically, your virtues and values are intertwined like a beautiful and intricately woven cord that strengthens your life. Trying to deny your personality by attempting to be something you're not is like pulling apart the strands of that cord—destroying both its strength and its beauty.

It's important to note here that there are no "bad" or "wrong" personality types. As I've described with the characteristics of each personality type, we all have areas in which we are especially gifted, as well as traits that can negatively affect our relationships (and our self-perception) if not handled with care. Revel in your uniqueness; it is the most precious gift you offer. At the same time, work to understand and honor others' unique personalities, so you can empower them to be themselves—that's the freedom we all need to thrive.

> **REVEL IN YOUR UNIQUENESS; IT IS THE MOST PRECIOUS GIFT YOU OFFER.**

In the next chapter, we'll focus on how to develop habits that will help you stay true to your identity and your personality.

WINNING ACTION: LIVE YOUR VIRTUES

How often do you do something simply because it's expected of you? You "grin and bear it" or bite your tongue...all the while feeling the internal conflict that exists when you live contrary to what is authentic to you.

The longer you live a life that is incongruent with your values, identity, and virtues, the more stressed and frustrated you will become. Isn't it time to bring your life into alignment and feel the freedom and power of being yourself?

For this exercise, I want you to examine what's behind the most stressful situations in your life. Could it be that there is a disconnect between who you are (your identity, your values, and especially your personality style) and your words and actions? Take a moment to consider the following questions:

- Do you feel that you are constantly asked to work outside your comfort zone?
- How often are you able to use your personality's strengths?
- How can you bring your gifts to the forefront of your work?

Happiness and harmony come when you shift your life so that you are drawing on your strengths, rather than operating outside of them and focusing on "fixing" your weaknesses.

Chapter 5

CREATE WINNING HABITS

"All our life, so far as it has definite form, is but a mass of habits."

-WILLIAM JAMES

When you get in your car, which do you do first: start the ignition or buckle your seat belt?

Can you remember?

Most people have to stop and think about the question. Go ahead. Envision yourself opening the car door, sitting down, and then...what comes next?

Every day, you repeat the same behavior, but I'll bet that when you get in your car, you give little to no thought to the process it takes to put the vehicle in motion. You just sit down, and within a few seconds you're cruising down the street.

Your daily routines—from the way you start your car, to the muscle movements required to walk, speak, and type, to the way you begin your morning—are largely automated. Much of your daily behavior (nearly half) is performed *habitually*.[29] *Habits*, as defined by *Merriam-Webster*, are a "usual way of behaving: Something that a person does often in a regular and repeated manner."

It's that "regular and repeated manner" that turns a behavior into a habit. After all, you didn't always know how to drive a car. You had to learn. At first, you deliberately thought about every single move you made. You precisely adjusted the seat and mirrors. You carefully checked your side and rearview mirrors. With perhaps a bit of struggle, you put the car into the correct gear. You checked your mirrors once more before applying pressure to the gas pedal. If the car lurched forward, you made a mental note, "*Not that hard!*" and tried again a bit more gently. Within a few weeks of daily driving, all those calculated movements felt like second nature. Now you no longer need to focus on your routine; you just do. Our brain's aptitude for forming habits is incredibly beneficial. We save time and energy because of our ability to instantly recall how to perform basic functions. For the brain, forming habits is somewhat self-serving; expending little to no energy focusing on mundane tasks frees you to talk to passengers, listen to the radio, and navigate new roads. (But please, don't text and drive!)

Habits are not inherently good or bad; they are simply your brain's way of conserving energy and minimizing conscious effort. And they can work for you or against you. Good habits, like brushing your teeth, exercising daily, meditating, and planning your daily schedule, can help you live a healthier, stronger, happier, and more productive life. Bad habits, like binge-watching your favorite shows, emotional eating, and procrastination, are self-sabotaging. Interestingly, you probably never intended to form those negative habits. They "just happened," or so it seems.

A habit is an automatic pattern of thought that leads to certain behaviors. When "running on automatic," there are many useful habits that streamline daily living. But to become unstoppable, you have to alter the way you approach what you do on a daily basis. You must be mindful and intentional about maximizing your time and energy. You must make choices consciously and conscientiously. You must think and act in harmony with your greatest aspirations. Don't let yourself fall asleep at the wheel by becoming the servant of your habits rather than their master.

There is no magic pill or one-time action that will erase all the bad habits you may have acquired. What you need are practical habit-redirecting techniques you can apply over time. A habit does not form instantaneously, neither will it be reformed instantaneously. However, if you are committed to becoming the next best version of yourself, determined to unleash the potential lying dormant inside of you, over time you will develop habits that are in sync with your greatness and point you toward your genius zone.

Humans are habit-forming creatures. We all have habits we should keep, and ones we would do better without. We must replace the ones that no longer serve the best version of ourselves if we intend to progress beyond our current realities and experience unstoppable success in life.

In his book, *The Power of Habit*, Charles Duhigg describes habits as powerful, but delicate:

> [Habits] can emerge outside of our consciousness, or can be deliberately designed. They often occur without our permission, but can be reshaped by fiddling with their parts. They shape our lives far more than we realize—they are so strong, in fact, that they cause our brains to cling to them at the exclusion of all else, including common sense.[30]

Isn't that the truth!? Even when you *know* a habit isn't helpful or productive, changing it requires focused and persistent effort. Common sense, or even willpower, isn't enough to change or break some habits. How many people do you know who have given up smoking more than once? How often have you committed to stop overeating or overspending? Somehow, when you're in the moment at the restaurant or store, stopping yourself never even crosses your mind! You may feel remorse or regret later, but common sense doesn't even show up until *after* the damage is done.

Yes, habits are powerful. As Duhigg notes, our habits shape our lives. And for that reason, you must shape your habits if you want to win at being unstoppable.

OUT WITH THE OLD, IN WITH THE NEW

Did you learn to ride a bicycle as a child? If so, you can probably hop on one today and within just a few seconds be pedaling your way around the block. Your brain tucked away all the habits necessary for staying balanced, steering, and braking. It might take several tries at it to feel fully confident, but before long, you will feel completely at ease. That's because our habits never really go away. They can be intentionally superseded, but they are never totally eliminated. When it comes to bicycling, or finding your way home after an extended vacation, those buried habits work to your advantage. The other side of that truth, however, means ingrained habits are always there to fall back on.

YOU MUST SHAPE YOUR HABITS IF YOU WANT TO WIN AT BEING UNSTOPPABLE.

"A nail is driven out by another nail; habit is overcome by habit."
-DESIDERIUS ERASMUS

Neural pathways formed by repetitive behaviors are like ruts in your brain. It is possible to climb out of those ruts and create new neural pathways with new repeated behaviors—but those old ruts remain. That's what makes attempts at simply eliminating bad habits so frustrating. Rationale and willpower may work for a few days, but before long, habitual behaviors will resurface and you'll end up back in that well-worn rut.

The way to win is to displace old habits by instilling new ones in their stead. In truth, creating a brand-new habit is easier than ridding yourself of an established one. In *The Compound Effect*, Darren Hardy recommends, "Think addition, not subtraction." When you try to eliminate a negative habit, your thoughts turn to what you *can't* or *shouldn't* do. That's like waving a red flag at a bull. Focusing on what you can't have makes you want it even more. Instead, focus on what you can have. Shift your attention to adding a positive habit to your life, rather than eliminating a negative one. Over time, you may discover that the undesirable habit gets replaced without much conscious thought or effort.

THE ANATOMY OF A HABIT

A rich man once asked an old, wise man to help his son change his bad habits. So, the wise man took the son on a walk through a garden. After taking a few steps, the wise man stopped and asked the young man to pluck a small flower from the ground. The young man reached down and easily pulled it out. The wise man nodded, and they resumed walking. A few moments later, they stopped again, and the wise man pointed toward another plant, a bit larger than the last. The young man firmly grabbed it, and with a bit of effort, pulled it from the ground. "Now, pull out that one," the wise man said, pointing toward a bush. The young man grabbed the bush with both hands and tugged with all of his strength, barely managing to pull it out of the ground. "Now, you see that small tree?" asked the wise man. "Try and pull it up." The young man grabbed the trunk with both hands and pulled as hard as he could, but he couldn't make it budge. "It's impossible!" he exclaimed. The wise man replied, "You see, my boy, it's the same with your habits. The longer you allow them to take root and grow in your life, the more difficult they become to pull out."[31]

Habits that don't serve our greatest good can become like weeds in our lives. They can proliferate until they choke out the effects of our good habits.

Understanding how habits work will allow you to, as Duhigg puts it, "fiddle with their parts." Researchers have found that our recurring daily activities are done in the same place, at the same time, and/or when we are in a particular mood.[32] That's because all habitual behaviors are initiated by a cue or **trigger**. The cue may be your alarm clock, or stress, or a particular smell, or a place (like your car or office desk). Whatever the cue is, it sets your routine into motion by sparking a craving or **desire** for an expected reward. Like Pavlov's dog responding to the dinner bell, when you smell your favorite foods, your mouth waters in anticipation of the delicious reward, *even when you are not hungry*. That craving pushes you into a routine **behavior** (aka habit) that ultimately satisfies the craving with a **reward**.

Trigger—>Desire—>Behavior—>Reward

Identifying your habits' triggers can help you anticipate and even circumvent routine behavior—but that requires conscious thought. Since habits are by nature performed subconsciously, attempting to catch and stop habitual behavior before it happens is challenging and improbable. As I said earlier, it's easier to create new habits than to change or eliminate old ones. So, I'm going to encourage you to use what you know about your core values and your personal goals to create new triggers that motivate new behaviors that will deliver the rewards you desire.

One more note about creating new habits: You must *believe* it's possible. If you need help changing a that's-just-the-way-I-am mindset, refer back to Chapter 1. You *can* most definitely change your life if you will choose to change your thinking.

HOW TO CREATE A NEW HABIT

It happens every January 1st. Resolutions are made, sometimes with great care and planning, and sometimes out of rash desperation. Promising to "be better this year" are common resolutions that include eating healthier, exercising more regularly, saving more, spending less, reading more, going to church, volunteering in the community, working smarter rather than harder, devoting more time to family—have I left anything out? By January 30, most of those good intentions have been replaced by feelings of disappointment and failure.

One of the most common mistakes people make when they are ready to win—when they have a "burning desire" to improve their lives—is to attempt to tackle a long list of *all* the aspects of their lives they want to change all at once.

Imagine trying to catch ten different balls simultaneously—all of which are being thrown at you from different angles. Could you catch one or two? Perhaps. But certainly not all of them, all at the same time. That's what it's like when you're trying to "fix" everything about your life in one fell swoop. It simply doesn't work.

Most of us have a few negative or self-defeating habits of which we are painfully aware. It's noble and good to recognize the areas of your life that need improvement. But for now, I'm going to ask you to focus on one. At the end of Chapter 3, I posed the crucial question: *What one thing can you change that will change everything?* If you're like most people, you know exactly what that one thing is. In the next

> START SMALL, CELEBRATE YOUR WINS, AND GIVE IT TIME.

few pages, I'm going to share some very practical ideas that will help you finally make that one big change that will change everything. Here's the plan: You're going to start small, celebrate your wins, and give it time. I know you can do it!

TINY HABITS

You already know that trying to make too many changes at once is a recipe for failure. Likewise, attempting to create a new routine by introducing a very difficult or time-consuming activity into your day sets you up for disappointment.

In his TED Talk, Stanford professor and behavior researcher Dr. B.J. Fogg explains that massive effort requires equally massive motivation. We've already noted that willpower won't win out over our established habits. And if those new habits require even *more* willpower, you're all but doomed to miss the mark. What does work are small, or as Fogg says, "tiny changes." *Tiny*, as in doing two push-ups or flossing one tooth, both examples Fogg offers in his TED Talk.[33]

Does flossing one tooth sound a bit simple...or perhaps ineffectual? Well, it certainly won't rid you of gingivitis right away, but Fogg insists that by doing one tiny behavior you create the habit of making time to floss. Once you're flossing one tooth regularly, the logical progression is to floss all of them eventually. It isn't flossing that is difficult; it is getting into the habit of doing it daily. "You need to design for the behaviors that lead to the outcomes," states Fogg.

How do you choose your tiny habit?

First, consider what reward you ultimately want. Go ahead and write down in your journal the one thing that could change everything.

Now, let's break down that outcome into small, incremental steps. Here's an example: Daniella is in sales. She knows that closing one additional client a week would propel her career and earn her and her family an all-expenses-paid vacation. What an outcome! However, closing the additional sale isn't the tiny habit. That's the outcome. Daniella's tiny habit might include calling one satisfied client a day to ask for a referral, or calling one prospect to schedule an appointment, or exchanging one business card with a new contact, or sending one follow-up email to just one person who said, "Let me think about it."

There are probably countless activities that could help you in your progress toward the ultimate outcome you desire. List at least five in your workbook or journal.

Review your list. Which of these activities do you already know how to do? If you don't know how to do any of them, which would be the easiest to learn? Which would require the least motivation? Pick that one, and only that one. Go for the little, *easy* wins.

Repeat.

And repeat again.

PULL THE TRIGGER...THEN CELEBRATE!

That sounds so simple, doesn't it? Pick one small thing and do it every day. Just do it.

Have you tried that before? Did it work?

If the "Just Do It!" slogan didn't work, you're going to want to pay attention to this next part of Fogg's Tiny Habits Model. It's brilliant.

Step 1: Create the Trigger

You've selected your tiny habit. Now you're going to create the trigger that motivates you to take action. Remember the sequence for habits:

Trigger—>Desire—>Behavior—>Reward

You need a prompt that tells your brain to perform the tiny action you've chosen. In Fogg's example about flossing, the trigger is brushing one's teeth. Initially, you're going to have to think about this trigger. It's not a habit—*yet*. Until it becomes so routine that you do it automatically, use Fogg's simple formula to remind yourself when to take action. It looks like this:

After I (existing behavior),

I will (new behavior).

So if the habit is flossing, you would say: "After I brush my teeth, I will floss one tooth."

For Daniella (the aforementioned salesperson), the tiny habit might be sending that follow-up email. But when? The key is to choose an existing, recurring behavior. Since things may get busier and less ordered throughout the day, as soon as she turns on her office computer in the morning, she will send that follow-up email. Her tiny habit statement would be: *After I turn on my computer, I will send one follow-up message to a prospect.*

Write down your trigger statement in your journal:

After I _____,

I will _____.

Step 2: Celebrate!

Behavior specialists and motivational experts across the board agree that behavioral changes happen when (and in all likelihood *because*) rewards are involved. No matter how intellectual we think we are, everyone likes a prize. We want to *feel* like winners! And the sooner, the better. That all-expense-paid vacation might be a good motivation for getting started, but without little rewards along the way, the brain loses interest. It craves that dose of dopamine that accompanies a reward...*now*!

For the sake of instant gratification, Fogg teaches his clients to cheer for themselves immediately after performing their tiny habit. A simple, "I'm awesome!" or a happy dance could be enough to get a shot of those celebratory endorphins.

After a week (or month) of successfully performing your new behavior, why not make the celebration a little bigger? Try a walk through the park, a luxurious bath, or dinner out with friends. "You've got to find little rewards to give yourself every month, every week, every day—even something small to acknowledge that you've held yourself to a new behavior,"[34] writes Darren Hardy in *The Compound Effect*.

Anticipation, researchers note, also increases motivation. So, decide now how you will celebrate your wins, both immediately and longer term. Then, enjoy the moments of your success! Congratulate yourself every time you take even the smallest step toward your goal.

GIVE IT TIME

The myth that people can acquire a new habit in twenty-one days is just that, a myth. We want to believe this myth because it doesn't seem too long or too difficult. But making real, lasting change takes longer and can be hard, but I bet you already knew that. In *Making Habits, Breaking Habits* psychologist and author Jeremy Dean cites a study conducted at the University College of London, which discovered that forming a new habit can take three times the mythical twenty-one days.[35] And depending on the difficulty of the habit, it could take even longer. "Although the study only covered eighty-four days . . . it turned out that some of the habits could have taken around 254 days to form—the better part of a year!"[36] Dean writes.

> *CONGRATULATE YOURSELF EVERY TIME YOU TAKE THE SMALLEST STEP TOWARD YOUR GOAL.*

Tiny habits, like drinking one extra glass of water a day, are easy enough to integrate. But more challenging activities, such as adding exercise to your schedule each day, take more time to feel so automatic that you do it without thinking. The lesson then is to make sure you give yourself an *abundance* of time to change your habit. After all, habits exist because you've spent years developing them. Remember the reality of neuroplasticity. Your repetitive choices create *physical* patterns (ruts) in your brain over a period of months, years, maybe even decades. Creating new neural pathways will take time and conscious, repeated action.

Don't expect overnight results as you try to form new habits. And *please*, don't berate yourself when you slip up and go back to the "old" way of doing things. It's going to happen. Accept that. When you fail, acknowledge that you allowed the autopilot to take over that day. Fire him (again) and get back into the captain's chair.

"The beauty of habits," writes Dean, "is that as they develop, they become more effortless. Even when you're tired, upset, or distracted, strong habits are likely to be performed because they're so ingrained." He adds:

> Habits that you've constructed yourself, for your own purposes, can seem like magic when they work. Like other behaviors that we carry out on a regular basis, the fruits of good habits may build up slowly, but they can repay the effort made to establish them many times over.[37]

WINNING ACTION: EVALUATE YOUR DESIRED OUTCOMES

Be honest. Identify one place in your life you've said you want to change, but haven't actualized that change yet. We all do it! *What goals have you made repeatedly, but failed to achieve?* Put that goal to the test:

1. Is it authentic? Did you make that goal because you wanted to please or impress someone?
2. If it is authentic, what is/are your barrier(s) to achieving it? What keeps getting in your way?
3. How can you overcome those barriers?

    •   Do you need a change of mindset?
    •   A change of environment?
    •   What tiny habits could push you toward your desired outcome?

Start small and work on one change at a time. When your daily actions support your goals and are in alignment with your values and virtues, you can be confident that you are on your winning path!

Chapter 6

TRANSPARENCY WINS EVERY TIME

"The best way to prove the clearness of your mind, is by showing its faults; as when a stream discovers the dirt at the bottom, it convinces us of the transparency and purity of the water."

—ALEXANDER POPE

"I'm not the most believable guy in the world right now," Lance Armstrong told Oprah in an interview, which aired on January 17, 2013. Nearly five months earlier, on August 24, 2012, the US Anti-Doping Agency banned the world-famous cyclist from all competitive sports and stripped him of the seven Tour de France titles he'd won between 1999 and 2005. During the interview, Armstrong admitted to having lied, adamantly and repeatedly, for more than a decade in regard to the allegations that he used performance-enhancing drugs. When Oprah asked Armstrong about a former teammate's accusation that he had forced or coerced his fellow riders to use steroids or other doping techniques by threatening their positions on the team, the first part of his response succinctly summed up his reality: "I'm not the most believable guy in the world right now."[38]

For years, Armstrong (and others around him) painstakingly crafted an image of athletic perfection. Winning felt good. Winning consecutive races felt even better. And when he came back to the sport after battling cancer, he says he was driven by a "ruthless and relentless win-at-all-costs attitude."[39] Ultimately, the price took him by surprise. His actions and the lies he'd so often repeated irreparably damaged his reputation as an athlete, as well as his legacy as the founder of the nonprofit Livestrong Foundation. Beyond those losses, his hubris and lack of transparency continue to taint every word he speaks. "I see the anger in people," Armstrong told Winfrey.

> And betrayal…and these are people that supported me, that believed in me, believed me—not just believed in me but believed what I was saying—and they have every right to feel betrayed, and it's my fault. I will spend the rest of my life—you know some people are gone forever—but I'll spend the rest of my life trying to earn back trust and apologize to people for the rest of my life.[40]

Lance Armstrong's story is extreme, although not uncommon. I've already mentioned Bernie Madoff in a previous chapter, and I'm sure you can think of a few politicians, tele-personalities, and celebrities who masterfully created an ideal public image. From the outside, everything looks perfect. It's a perfectly engineered glass-house brand, until someone—a spouse, a reporter, a blogger, an activist—throws a stone, and the glass shatters.

WHAT DOES TRANSPARENCY MEAN?

You may not believe that you and Lance Armstrong have anything in common. After all, he rationalized illegal and unethical behavior for years. That's not you. But look at his reason and perhaps you can begin to relate. What drove him to cheat, lie, and slander those who called him on his actions? In a word, *pride*. Because, as he said in the interview with Winfrey, he was "trying to perpetuate the story and hide the truth."[41]

Perpetuating the story and hiding the truth.

Let's take this concept of deception down a notch to something that's a bit more relevant. Take a few moments to consider these questions:

1. Why do you wear the clothes you wear?
2. How do you choose which pictures and words to post on social media?
3. What brand of watch do you wear?
4. What's truly beneath that smile?
5. In what passive-aggressive activities do you engage?
6. Do you rush to tidy up your house before people come to visit?
7. How do you want to be perceived by your family members, friends, co-workers, clients, acquaintances, and the general public?
8. Have you intentionally left out facts and details and chalked it up to "privacy"?

To some extent, all (or at least the majority) of us purposefully design the image we present to others. Truly, that in and of itself is not the problem. In the coming chapters, we'll discuss how your personal brand and public reputation can be powerful assets; you want to shape them carefully and deliberately. But here is the key: What you present to others—from your closest confidant to the stranger who sees your Twitter feed—should be authentic.

AUTHENTICITY MUST WRAP AROUND AND TRAVEL THROUGH EVERY ASPECT OF YOUR BEING AND EVERY AREA OF YOUR LIFE.

There's that word again. *Authentic.* Do you see how authenticity must wrap around and travel through every aspect of your being and every area of your life? Transparent living isn't simply about honesty, although that honorable trait is essential.

Transparency, at least for our purposes, is about being who you are—inside and out.

"The way to gain a good reputation is to endeavor to be how you desire to appear."
-SOCRATES

In the wake of financial and business fallouts, consumers and law-makers demand transparency and accountability. We all want to know that those in positions of power are following through on their promises and performing ethically. We implement complex systems of checks and balances in our businesses, banks, and government to keep operations "above board." Some people resent those demands for public visibility into their organization's inner workings. Others, like social marketer Pat Flynn, jump aboard the transparency bandwagon—using their openness to increase trust and profits.[42] While some in his industry avoid giving specifics on their operations, Flynn posts his earnings, and explains his methods as well as his successes and failures on his blog. Ultimately, that willingness to share earns his customers' trust, as well as their business.

Perhaps Flynn, and other social media leaders like author and entrepreneur Gary Vaynerchuk and Facebook CEO Mark Zuckerberg, are intentional about their transparency because they understand that in today's tech-driven world, the divide between our public and private lives no longer exists. If your life is inauthentic, others will eventually know the truth. Rather than hiding, they opt to control the story by telling it themselves.

As we think about transparency, the goal isn't to paint a façade of the perfect life, nor is it to go to the other extreme and publicly air all your dirty laundry. The point is to be yourself—your best self—whether you are alone at home, posting online, or standing in front of a crowd. If you have dirty laundry (and we all do), there's no need to flaunt it. But you must deal with it honestly. That means telling the appropriate people, owning up to your faults, and working to amend mistakes. And for goodness' sake, don't lie. I promise you this: Hiding dirty laundry in a closet only creates a bigger stink.

Like it or not, and ready or not, transparency is part of our world today. For it to work for you, rather than against you, you must continually ask the question: Are my actions and words in alignment with who I really want to be? If not, your responsibility is to work on bringing integrity—*or congruency*—to your life. I'll discuss some specific ways to do that shortly. But first, let's take a look at why we try to hide.

FEAR: THE TRUTH BEHIND WHY WE HIDE

FEAR: False Evidence Appearing Real.

I once heard a story about the irrational nature of fear that goes like this:

> There was a lion who feared nothing except the crowing of cocks. A chill would go down his spine whenever he heard a cock crowing. One day, he confessed his fear to the elephant, who was greatly amused. "How can the crowing of a cock hurt you?" he asked the lion. "Think about it!" Just then a mosquito began circling the elephant's head, frightening him out of his wits. "If it gets into my ear I'm doomed!" he shrieked, flailing at the insect with his trunk. Now it was the lion's turn to feel amused. The moral of the story: If we could see our fears as others see them, we would realize that most of our fears make no sense![43]

The power fear holds can seem immense, intense, and unbreakable. Fear can cause us to act in ridiculous ways and even contradict our own standards and values. It can push us to excel, or it can paralyze us. If we allow it, it can drive us to do the unimaginable. But don't believe for a second that fear's power is unbreakable. That's a lie; it's another case of false evidence appearing real.

In *Happy This Year*, Will Bowen makes the claim that fear is behind every lie. I think he's probably right! People lie because they are afraid of:

- The fallout that comes with telling the truth
- Taking responsibility for their behavior
- Having uncomfortable conversations
- Being left
- Missing out
- Losing a job, influence, credibility, or a relationship
- Having people compare them unfavorably to others
- Disappointing people
- Failing[44]

Some people even lie to themselves because they're afraid of succeeding!

Fear leads to deception and to an inauthentic and guarded life that is at risk of collapsing like a house of cards. To bring clarity back into our lives, we must search within to discover and deal with the specific fears that cause us to hide.

FEAR OF FAILING

There is perhaps no fear more common than that of failure. Don't we all want to succeed—to win?

Unfortunately, the fear of failing too often stops people from even trying. Their belief is that by failing, they'll be disgraced.

Perhaps you remember all too clearly the pain and awkwardness of middle school, when slipups might as well have been broadcast from the loudspeaker. It seemed all eyes were on you the moment you made a mistake. Everyone knew when your boyfriend dumped you for another girl. The "real" athletes teased you because you weren't talented enough to make the sports team. Tripping up the stairs quite literally stopped your "friends" in their tracks just long enough to point and laugh.

Thankfully, those days are long gone for most of us. Consciously we know that no one is likely to point and laugh at our mistakes or failures. Even so, the desire to impress people with our abilities and achievements is intense. If this particular fear causes you to look outward—to see what others are doing and how you fail to measure up—your focus is on the wrong thing.

> "A failure is not always a mistake; it may simply be the best one can do under the circumstances. The real mistake is to stop trying."
>
> -B. F. SKINNER

Where is your focus? Is it on impressing others? Or is it on living to the best of your ability with integrity? Are you more concerned with winning against others or with growing personally?

Lance Armstrong cheated and lied because his focus was on winning the race. Losing seemed unthinkable; he was afraid of failure. In the end, that fear was his undoing. He lost the titles he'd won and an estimated seventy-five million dollars in future income when his sponsors dropped him.[45] More importantly, his fear of failure cost him his reputation and relationships.

> ACKNOWLEDGE AND EVEN REVEL IN THE TRUTH THAT THERE ARE THINGS ONLY YOU CAN DO.

Remember: You are an original. To compete with yourself and win, you must acknowledge and even *revel* in the truth that there are things only you can do—and the world is waiting on you to do them! And here's the truth: You may try and fail. That, too, is good. Failure teaches you how to improve. It challenges you to grow. Motivational speaker and author Tony Robbins explains that failure is an invaluable part of the growth process: "I've come to believe that all my past failure and frustration were actually laying the foundation for the understandings that have created the new level of living I now enjoy."[46]

FEAR OF WHAT OTHERS THINK

"You wouldn't worry so much about what others think of you,
if you realized how seldom they do."

-ELEANOR ROOSEVELT

What will they think of me? This very common fear could cover an extremely broad spectrum of "others." For instance, it's common, yet unnecessary, to concern yourself with what strangers or even your four hundred "friends" on Facebook think about you. The reality is, they are probably not thinking about you at all. Humans, as a rule, don't think about much beyond themselves and their immediate sphere of influence. Our brains don't have the patience or band-width to focus on things that are not immediately important to us. So, let's limit the focus of this discussion to what the people closest to you think. Really, those are the people who matter most to you. And it's in these relationships that a lack of transparency, honesty, and authenticity can do the worst damage. As you'll learn in the next few pages, we must be willing to be vulnerable—to risk sharing our true selves with others if our marriages, friendships, and relation-ships with our parents and children are going to survive and thrive.

I want you to carefully consider the people you allow into your circle of influence. We are shaped by those with whom we surround ourselves. If someone you spend time with regularly demands that you live up to an expectation that you have not set for yourself, per-haps it's time to evaluate the quantity of time you devote to that relationship. If the goal for your life is authenticity, it is crucial that you feel free to be yourself—and that you allow others that same freedom.

To close this section, I want to remind you that you are *enough*. Life is not about living up to society's expectations—or even those of your parents or spouse. Neither is it about competing with others. It is about becoming the best version of yourself. I love how Brené Brown explains this journey toward what she calls "wholehearted living"—which in many ways is about living transparently. In her book *The Gifts of Imperfection*, she writes:

> Wholehearted living is about engaging in our lives from a place of worthiness. It means cultivating the courage, compassion, and connection to wake up in the morning and think, "*No matter what gets done and how much is left undone, I am enough.*" It's going to bed at night thinking, "*Yes, I am imperfect and vulnerable and sometimes afraid, but that doesn't change the truth that I am also brave and worthy of love and belonging.*"[47]

Determine to be brave enough to be yourself.

HOW AND WHY TO BE TRANSPARENT

"When we consistently betray ourselves,
we can expect to do the same to the people we love."

-BRENÉ BROWN

Have you ever had the experience of being completely duped by someone? Have you had a friend, co-worker, or spouse break your confidence by withholding or manipulating information? How did you feel when you discovered the lies?

If you've been on the receiving end of dishonesty, you know how destructive that break of trust can be to your relationships. Even "little white lies," which in and of themselves may seem unimport-ant, can break down levels of trust. The reason: The person who was lied to wonders, "If he or she lied about something so small, why would they tell the truth if there were real consequences?"

TRANSPARENCY AT HOME

The truth is, any lack of honesty can be destructive to your relationships, as well as to your physical, emotional, and mental health. Here's a telling story that illustrates how self-destructive mistruths can be:

> One day, a boy and a girl were playing together. The boy had a collection of marbles. The girl had some sweets with her. The boy told the girl that he would give her all his marbles in exchange for her sweets. The girl agreed. The boy kept the biggest and most beautiful marble aside and gave the rest to the girl. The girl gave him all her sweets as she had promised. That night, the girl slept peacefully. But the boy lay awake wondering if the girl had hidden the best sweet from him the way he had hidden his best marble.[48]

In *Happy This Year*, Will Bowen cites a study conducted at the University of Notre Dame in which researchers evaluated the influence dishonesty had on the participants' health and relationships. One group was instructed not to lie at all during the ten-week study. If they couldn't bring themselves to tell the truth, they were encouraged to simply remain silent. The other group received no instruction about lying. Using weekly polygraph tests, the researchers then assessed how often each of the participants lied. "The results were impressive and significant," Bowen writes. "The group that was asked to forgo telling lies reported fewer mental health issues, such as anxiety and sadness, as well as fewer physical ailments, such as headaches and sore throats. In addition, the group that was instructed not to lie during the ten-week experiment reported improvements in their close personal relationships."[49]

Isn't it interesting that although people often lie because they are afraid of damaging their relationships, the research shows that truth brings people together?

Think about some of the habitual lies people express as nonchalant sound bites:

"Just kidding!"
"Tell me the truth, I won't be mad."
"I'm fine."
"I'll call you later."
"I don't remember."
"My phone died."
"My computer crashed."
"I never got the email. It must have gone to spam."
"I wish I could be there, but I've got an appointment/recital/funeral."
"Sorry I'm late, there was an accident."

By committing to honesty and authenticity, we strengthen the most important relationships in our lives. Indeed, honesty and authenticity can be a conduit to stronger, more enjoyable connections. "We cultivate love when we allow our most vulnerable and powerful selves to be deeply seen and known—and when we honor the spiritual connection that grows from that offering with trust, respect, kindness and affection,"[50] writes Brené Brown.

> BY COMMITTING TO HONESTY AND AUTHENTICITY, WE STRENGTHEN THE MOST IMPORTANT RELATIONSHIPS IN OUR LIVES.

Another study conducted at Ohio State University offers additional evidence that both authenticity and transparency work to our benefit. The study revealed that men and women who were true to themselves also tended to be more intimate and able to share and interact with their partners. In addition to feeling positive about their relationships, these authentic and transparent individuals reported greater personal well-being. The reasoning behind all these benefits of transparency, says the lead author of the study, Amy Brunell, supports the need for people to know themselves well. "If you're true to yourself, it is easier to act in ways that build intimacy in relationships, and that's going to make your relationship more fulfilling."[51]

ON THE SOCIAL FRONT

There's a whole wide world beyond our close, personal relationships, a world that technology, and specifically social media, brings us into contact with on a daily, sometimes minute-by-minute, basis.

Unfortunately, many of the connections we have through social media are superficial. It's a paradox that with all our friends, fans, and followers, deep connections are extremely rare. Despite our increased online networks, most people have only two confidants.[52]

"In the silence of connection, people are comforted by being in touch with a lot of people—carefully kept at bay," says Sherry Turkle, author of *Alone Together: Why We Expect More from Technology and Less from Each Other*:

> We can't get enough of one another if we can use technology to keep one another at distances we can control: Not too close, not too far, just right. I think of it as a Goldilocks effect. Texting and e-mail and posting let us present the self we want to be. This means we can edit. And if we wish to, we can delete. Or retouch: The voice, the flesh, the face, the body. Not too much, not too little—just right.[53]

Perhaps it is this editing that prevents real connection. This lack of transparency creates unrealistic expectations about how our lives should look. Perfect people, perfectly decorated houses, perfectly coiffed hairstyles (how many selfies have you seen or posted after a new do?), happy children, happy couples—outsiders seeing our Facebook threads—would have no idea of the hardships, hurts, and reality we struggle through.

All that perfection can be problematic. When you present an image people know they can't compare or relate to, they distance themselves. The lack of transparency perpetuates the myth of perfection. Others assume we hold them to the same standard of (false) perfection.

> "When we don't give ourselves permission to be free, we rarely tolerate that freedom in others. We put them down, make fun of them, ridicule their behaviors, and sometimes shame them. We can do this intentionally or unconsciously."
>
> -BRENÉ BROWN

Remember, it is your responsibility to bring integrity and congruency into your life. You can do this by allowing people to see the real you. You've already done the self-discovery work. You know the kind of person you want to be. You know what your core values and your virtues are. As we close out this section, I want to encourage you to be true to yourself and be honest with others in the way you represent yourself. Don't deny who you are so that you can fit in or paint the perfect image. The bravery you display by living authentically and transparently will empower others to do the same.

WINNING ACTION: CREATING CONGRUENCY

Ask: "Are my actions and words in alignment with who I really want to be?" If not, what do you need to change? What will you change today?

- Is there any area of your life that feels incongruent? For example, do your Facebook posts share only picture-perfect moments?

- Are you presenting an image that seems "too good to be true"? Remember that doing so can make you unapproachable, which can hamper your ability to influence others effectively.

It's impossible to win if you're attempting to live behind a false front. As you've seen in the examples presented in this chapter, people who pretend to be something they're not risk—and lose—far more than they bargain for. Being who you are *all the time* eliminates the risk of being "found out." Beyond that, there's immeasurable peace that comes from not having to hide or pretend. Be brave enough to be yourself and discover the unstoppable power within.

BE BRAVE ENOUGH TO BE YOURSELF AND DISCOVER THE UNSTOPPABLE POWER WITHIN.

SECTION THREE
WINFLUENCE

> "Because everything we say and do is the length and shadow of our own souls,
> our influence is determined by the quality of our being."
>
> ~DALE TURNER

We began this personal-transformation process with self-discovery—*learning who you are*. With that crucial knowledge in mind, the next step was to better understand how (and why)—to *be true to yourself, your personality, your goals, and your relationships*. Now it's time to take the next step and *share who you are with others*, for their benefit and yours.

You see, this journey isn't simply about improving your life; it's also making a difference in the world around you. The greater your sphere of influence, the greater the impact you make on the world, and the more unstoppable you will become. That's why this section is devoted to expanding your capacity to influence.

First, you'll learn what influence is and how it should and shouldn't be used. You'll also learn strategies for connecting with others in honest and meaningful ways.

Then we'll look at how you can intentionally and authentically craft a brand that further increases your ability to become a powerful influencer. You'll learn how to set yourself apart in a highly competitive marketplace and make yourself memorable to those you meet.

YOUR CREDIBILITY IS THE CURRENCY YOU USE TO GROW YOUR SOCIAL CAPITAL.

As we close out this section, we'll look at one of the most critical aspects of your reputation: credibility. All the work you put into designing a brand and making a difference in others' lives can be erased with a single poor choice or rashly spoken word. Don't allow that to happen! Your credibility is the currency you use to grow your social capital. The final chapter in this section will show you how to cultivate and maintain unstoppable credibility.

Let's get started!

Chapter 7

WIN THROUGH INFLUENCE

"Individually, we are one drop. Together, we are an ocean."

-RYUNOSUKE SATORO

In the 1950s, American television audiences thrilled to the adventures of the Lone Ranger. As he tamed the Wild West, this mysterious masked man embodied a time when a pistol, a horse, and a trusted sidekick were all anyone needed to save the day. The image of this solitary rider became an enduring icon in American culture, but it is a far cry from the reality of modern life.

We live in a time when people are more connected than ever. Smartphones and social media provide real-time updates on the most mundane or monumental aspects of daily life. While popular culture may idealize the image of the Lone Ranger, modern life pushes us to stay engaged. To deny this fact is to cut yourself off from the resources and relationships you need to thrive. Because whether you realize it or not yet, you *do* need others in order to win.

You've heard the adage, "It's not what you know, but who you know that counts." I might add that *who knows you* matters a great deal, as well. But be aware of what it means to "know" people. As I mentioned in the previous chapter, social media presents a paradoxical problem. While our online stats (friends, followers, and fans) may indicate huge networks, the reality is that many (if not most) of those connections are superficial and thereby ineffective. More than the *quantity* of connections in your network, your suc-

YOUR SUCCESS DEPENDS UPON YOUR ABILITY TO POSITIVELY INFLUENCE OTHERS.

cess depends upon your ability to *positively influence* others. As John C. Maxwell and Jim Dornan explain in their book *How to Influence People,* "If your desire is to be successful or to make a positive impact on your world, you need to become a person of influence. Without influence, there is no success."[54]

WHAT IS INFLUENCE?

Influence is your ability to affect the behavior of another person without forcing them into action. Influence isn't about command-ing or directing people from a position of power. Nor is it about coercion or manipulation.

To some degree, we all have influence over—and are influenced by—others. It happens naturally when we spend time with people. You shop where your friends shop. You read what your friends read. Your children follow the traditions you learned from your parents. No one made you do those things; you are simply modeling learned behavior. (That's why it's so important to be intentional about the people with whom you surround yourself!) But becoming a "person of influence"—one who makes a purposeful, positive impact on others' lives—requires intentionality, and it happens in incremental stages.

In *How to Influence People,* Maxwell and Dornan explain the four-stage progression in the significance or amount of influence you have with others. As you move through these stages with a person, your relationship becomes more meaningful and benefi-cial—to both parties.

Model —> Motivate —> Mentor —> Multiply

As you read about each stage, I want you to do two things:

1. Watch for our winning themes: authenticity, integrity, and transparency. The best way to influence people is by knowing who you are, being who you are, and sharing who you are. If at any point you slip into pretending to be someone or something other than your authentic self, your lack of integrity will damage, if not eradicate, your capacity to influence.

2. Think about the people in your life and the depth of relationship you have with them. How might you move with those people from one stage to the next?

Model: "People are first influenced by what they see," explain Maxwell and Dornan. Before people accept your influence in their lives, they will watch to see if your words and actions are congruent. To earn the right to influence another person's life, you must first model (show) your worthiness through your own authentic behavior, words, and results.

Motivate: "You become a motivational influencer when you encourage people and communicate with them on an emotional level," write Maxwell and Dornan. Only when you connect with people in meaningful ways can you expect to move them to action. Making that connection requires time, transparency, and trust. You must invest time in your relationships and demonstrate yourself to be who you say you are over and over again.

Mentor: The next stage of influence comes when you take motivation to a higher, more personal level. Maxwell and Dornan define *mentoring* as: "Pouring your life into other people and helping them reach their potential." At this stage, you invite people to look behind the curtain to see how to achieve what you've achieved.

Multiply: "As a multiplying influencer, you help people to become positive influencers in the lives of others and pass on not only what they have received from you, but also what they have learned and gleaned on their own," write Maxwell and Dornan. As you might expect, developing this level of influence requires significant time, communication, and care. It is also how you can create a legacy, something we'll discuss more in Chapter 11.

Increasing your influence is about the difference you make in the lives of others. The process begins with one-to-one relationships that are developed and nurtured over time. As the depth of those relationships increase, so does your circle of influence. Each time you reach the "Multiply" stage with a new person, you then have the ability to influence that person's network, as well. Person by person, you can make a positive impact on the world.

CHECK YOUR MOTIVES

"People will forget what you said, people will forget what you did,
but people will never forget how you made them feel."
-MAYA ANGELOU

Have you ever desperately wanted a specific person to be your friend? It might have been a childhood classmate who played fun games at recess or the cool girl at school whom all of the boys noticed. You might have thought, "If I could just sit at her table at lunchtime, the other kids will think I'm cool, too." Or maybe you wanted to befriend a colleague who had the kind of professional connections you could only dream of, or a wealthy uncle whom you hoped would share the spoils of his riches. Whatever the reason, you longed for what these relationships could give you.

That longing reflects a common desire. Because we are made for relationships, a healthy drive pushes us to connect with others. However, at times, our motivation isn't so pure. Author Donald Miller asks anyone who longs for relationship an important question: "Do we love because we love, or do we love in order to be loved? The first [question] is pure, the second isn't any more selfless than not loving at all."[55]

Miller gets to the heart of the issue: At times we desire relationships for what they can give us, rather than for what we can give to the other person. It's critical to remember that your ability to influence others starts with understanding that you need others—*and that others need you.* The goal is to establish and nurture mutually beneficial relationships.

Selfish motives are easily apparent and end up turning others off. They impair our judgment, and because of the distrust they create, they can impair our ability to influence. Having the right motives is vital to the health of any relationship. Unfortunately, it's far easier to guess at other people's motives than to recognize and admit to our own. We simply watch their behavior and make assumptions about the reasons behind their actions. Our assumptions may or may not be correct; nevertheless, we make judgments about the person based on what we believe about their motives.

Guess what? Others are doing the same thing—making judgments about *your* motives. That's why being aware of what drives your behavior is critical. The truth is that just as you are responsible for your actions, you are accountable for your motives. And just as it is possible to change your mindset, it is possible to develop positive motives. To determine the right way to relate, it's helpful to understand how unhealthy motives might look:

- **You may pursue relationships to fill a need in your life.** Loving relationships can fill legitimate needs in your life, like the need for companionship, to collaborate, or to accomplish what one person cannot accomplish alone. However, if you seek relationships because you feel lonely, bored, or insecure, you may be exploiting the other person. Miller explains, "When we love in order to get security, the person we love is just being used."

- **You may cultivate relationships for what they can give you.** Maybe you value a friend's social connections, status, or clout. Authentic relationships are mutually beneficial, but with impure motives you value what the relationship gives you more than you value the person.
- **You may use relationships to distract you from other areas of your life.** Nothing keeps your mind off a problem like staying busy. Financial worries? Enjoy a night on the town with the girls and pretend like nothing is wrong. Fighting with your wife? Spend more time at the basketball court playing pick-up with your friends. Healthy relationships provide valuable stress relief, but with unhealthy motivation, they merely distract you from the deeper issues in your life. Which is unfortunate for your friend or partner; you can't be fully attentive to their needs when you're using the relationship as a distraction.

How can you be sure to develop pure motives in your relationships?

- **Put others first.** This practice goes against human nature, but making it your motive can serve you well. As author and speaker Zig Ziglar said so often, "You will get all you want in life, if you help enough other people get what they want."[56] If you really want to win, put others first. Never view yourself as the most important person in the relationship.
- **Find joy in giving without expecting anything in return.** Transactions are an everyday part of our lives. We exchange money for services and products all day long. We trade and barter and haggle—and we almost always get something in return for our money, time, or effort. But this level of giving is different. Influencers seek transformation rather than transaction. To change this pervasive expectation for a "fair trade," deter-

INFLUENCERS SEEK TRANSFORMATION RATHER THAN TRANSACTION.

mine to begin giving something of yourself *without* requiring, asking, or *desiring* any form of payment. Look for opportunities to help people who have no way of repaying you. Dale Carnegie, author of the famed *How to Win Friends and Influence People*, describes the feeling you will get when you give of yourself unselfishly without anticipating any reward as one "that flows and sings in your memory long after the incident is past."[57]

- **Stop looking to others for approval.** I hope that as you worked through the self-discovery portions of the life-transformation process, you began to address the need to impress others. In truth, as you become intentional about living authentically, the craving for others' approval diminishes. The reason for this is that you begin to experience the reality that giving your best, truest self to the world is more beneficial—and satisfying—than trying to fit into anyone else's mold.

Take some time to evaluate the relationships you value and check your motives.

Why are you drawn to each of those people?

Are you seeking to get, or to give?

Are you more concerned with what the other person can do for you than with what you can bring to the relationship?

If you want to become a person of influence, you must stop viewing your relationships as transactional and start looking for ways you can improve or even transform the other person's life.

WHOM DO YOU INFLUENCE?

"Relationships are all there is. Everything in the universe only exists because it is in relationship to everything else. Nothing exists in isolation. We have to stop pretending we are individuals that can go it alone."

-MARGARET WHEATLEY

At the moment of your birth, you joined the constellation of relationships that connects all human beings; from the doctor who grasped your slippery newborn feet, to your mother who pulled you to her chest, to the neighbor who welcomed your parents home from the hospital—each encounter introduced you to a lifetime of interaction with others.

Each of us lives within a "relational constellation," a vast network of people that flows from our most intimate, personal relationships through to our business and civic associations, and ultimately to the world at large.

As we've already seen, influence does not happen without relationships. By evaluating your current connections, you can see where and with whom you currently have the most impact. There are five categories of people in your relational constellation, ranging from distant acquaintances to your most personal connections. As you take a broad look at these categories, you may be surprised and encouraged by the wealth of relationships you possess. Look for gaps in your network, and identify people with whom you'd like to establish a stronger connection either personally or professionally. Realize that the stronger your connections are, the greater your capacity to influence.

THE 5 MOST IMPORTANT CATEGORIES OF RELATIONAL NETWORKS

1. **Your Database:** This refers to everyone whom you consider a "contact." These are people you've interacted with by email, phone, Instagram, Facebook, Pinterest, or Twitter. You may have met them at speaking engagements, or in the community. You may have simply acquired their business card at an event or been referred to them by a friend or colleague. This will be your largest group of relationships. These people may know your name and title. Even if they don't know much

about you, they have an impression of your reputation and have probably already determined whether they think you are "real" and trustworthy.

2. **Your Network:** This category refers to specific subgroups of people with whom you share an affinity or with whom you share a greater degree of trust. For example, you might belong to a university alumni group, participate in a business network, attend church together, or frequent the same social events. These people know enough about you that (if they respect you) they would be willing to offer a personal recommendation for your work. Networks rarely exceed two hundred contacts. To determine if someone is in your network, ask yourself, "Would this person return my phone call in a timely manner?"

3. **Your Inner Circle:** This category describes people who will give you candid feedback about your personal life or career. You need trustworthy, honest people in your inner circle who will push you to be your best. These relationships are mutually beneficial, purpose-driven, achievement-focused, value-adding, collaborative, and supportive. And because they know and like you, they are the people you can count on to lend a hand. The people in your inner circle may fluctuate, but ideally you will have from twenty to thirty people in this category.

4. **Advisors or Mentors:** These are the five or six people who keep an eye on your life and whom you trust to provide direction and "redirection" when necessary. These are the individuals who will give you solid advice, perspective, and counsel—who will hold you accountable for maximizing your potential while living true to your core values. They are the people who care how you are doing as a whole person.

5. **Friends and Family:** Your most significant relationships are the people closest to you. These are the people who know you best and will walk with you through any circumstance.

Think back to our discussion on transparency in the previous chapter. How you present yourself in social media determines how your database—your largest group of contacts—sees you. The people in your network have probably seen you in enough social settings to get a feel for your authenticity. Those who know the "real you," your inner circle, mentors, family members, and close friends, should see no disconnect between your public face and your private life.

As you evaluate your relationship constellation, consider where you fit into others' constellations. Do people know and trust you enough to call on you for help or advice? Are you authentic and approachable enough that those in your network would feel comfortable reaching out to you?

Gathering a circle of trustworthy, talented people around you will open doors to new opportunities, raise the level of your game, and provide support in a time of need. But don't believe the myth that your influence is determined solely by the number of people in your database. The quality of your relationships is as valuable, if not more so, than the quantity of contacts in your phone. "You don't have to have big names in your network. You don't need Warren Buffett's Rolodex to be successful in life," counsels Liz Lynch, author of *Smart Networking*. "Rather than pine for the network you don't have, appreciate and leverage the one you do have." Instead of attempting to build a network with strangers, develop more significant connections with the people you know. People will be more motivated to listen to, support, and follow you if they already have a relationship with you.

HOW TO INFLUENCE POSITIVELY AND EFFECTIVELY

"If we want to make friends, let's put ourselves out to do things for other people—things that require time, energy, unselfishness, and thoughtfulness."

-DALE CARNEGIE

Clearly, relationships are where your influence begins. You can build neither overnight. In their book *Career Distinction*, William Arruda and Kirsten Dixson stress the importance of building relationships *before* you need them: "When someone comes to me for advice on how to build a network because they need a job now, I tell them it's useless. People can tell the difference between desperation and an earnest attempt to create a relationship."[58] (That's why it's so important to check your motives!)

> RELATIONSHIPS ARE WHERE YOUR INFLUENCE BEGINS.

To Be Interesting to Others, Be Interested IN Others

"The royal road to a person's heart is to talk about the things he or she treasures most," wrote Dale Carnegie. It's important to note he didn't say, "Pretend to be interested in others." To have real influence with others, they must feel that you *genuinely* care about them. If you're pretending to like them or only half-listen as they speak, they will see right through you—and there goes any shot of making a positive difference in their lives. So what if you're not interested in the things they like to talk about? Listen anyway! Listening to others and engaging them in conversation shows that you care about the *person* to whom you are speaking.

ADD VALUE TO PEOPLE'S LIVES

People want to be around someone who adds value to their relationships. You can increase the quality of life for those around you by offering tangible (concrete) value or intangible (relational/emotional) value.

To add **tangible value**, help people GET something. You might:

- Connect prospective buyers with sellers;
- Introduce someone to a potential business partner;
- Recommend a friend for a job;

- Gather information on a colleague's behalf;
- Counsel someone as they make a decision; or
- Provide access to people, places, or experiences.

To add **intangible value**, help people FEEL something. You can:

- Provide support. Let people know you have their back and can be called upon in a time of need;
- Express gratitude to make people feel appreciated; or
- Regularly interact: See people on a regular basis to deepen your relationship and create opportunities to encourage one another.

Influencers desire the best for the people in their lives, and they generously share resources, relationships, and support.

STOP KEEPING SCORE

Katherine Graham never intended to become a publisher, but when her husband, Phillip Graham, died suddenly in 1963, she assumed his role as head of the *Washington Post*, one of the nation's leading newspapers. Skeptical onlookers questioned the shy widow's ability to run the company, but over the next twenty years, she became one of the most powerful women in journalism.

As she moved in the city's most elite social circles, Katherine Graham gained a reputation as a gracious, stylish hostess; however, she's best remembered for her ability to connect with people from any walk of life. From the women who cleaned the *Post*'s offices to the men who ran the newspaper presses, she made friends with everyone, regardless of their ability to advance her own social standing.

In his book, *Never Eat Alone*, Keith Ferrazzi reflects on Graham's diverse social connections: "[Her relationships] reveal an inner truth about the skill of reaching out to others: Those who are best at it don't network—they make friends. They gain admirers and win trust precisely *because* their amicable overtures extend to everyone. A widening circle of influence is an unintended result, not a calculated one."[59]

MAKE IT YOUR GOAL TO DEVELOP MUTUALLY BENEFICIAL RELATIONSHIPS.

As Graham's life reveals, influencers take an interest in the lives and welfare of others. This "others-orientation" sets the tone for all their relationships, and ultimately drives their success.

Make it your goal to develop mutually beneficial relationships. Determine to be known as someone who gives generously of their time and energy. Develop a reputation as a person who genuinely cares about others and their success. When you make people feel important, they will welcome your insights and guidance—and they'll be happy to connect you with others in their circles.

Person by person, you can increase your sphere of influence and your ability to make a positive impact on the world. In the next chapter, we'll look at how your personal brand (Yes, you have one!) supports or hinders your success as an influencer.

WINNING ACTION: *ASK FOR FEEDBACK*

Our ability to gauge how others view us is faulted at best. Your mentors, close friends, and family members can help shed light on how you come across in conversation—both online and in person.

IMPORTANT: Before you ask someone for their honest feedback, commit to them (and to yourself) to accept their comments without argument. This isn't a time for justifying why you behave the way you do.

The goal of this exercise is to understand how your actions, attitudes, and words make others feel.

1. Am I a good listener?

2. What, if anything, do I do that makes you feel that I'm not fully engaged in our conversations?

3. What do you think motivates me?

4. Are my real life and my online profiles congruent?

5. In what areas of my life do you feel that I present myself as less than 100 percent authentic?

Chapter 8

BRAND TO WIN

"The keys to brand success are self-definition, transparency, authenticity, and accountability."

-SIMON MAINWARING

Do clothes make the woman, or does the woman make the clothes?

Lady Diana, the "people's princess," knew how to captivate a room. From her fashion to her humanitarian activism, she changed the world while fulfilling her royal duties to England. She was married to power, but became a more powerful brand than her husband or the royal house he represented. Although her husband was born into an institution that commands influence, Diana became more influential. She developed an irresistible brand that impacted the entire world, separate and apart from her husband or his family.

Lady Diana redefined the definition of elegance. She represented all that was good in humanity and the importance of social interaction. By being the first celebrity photographed with HIV patients, she broke the stigma. She led with a smile and possessed empathy at a time when people needed it most. "She has a sympathetic face," her father once said, "the sort that you can't help but trust."[60]

In the 1980s, AIDS arrived on the world stage. It was a death sentence for those who contracted the virus; a new, frightening disease because there was no known cure for it. People believed you could catch AIDS from touching someone who had it. Ignorance fueled such fear, that the shame and shunning was nearly worse than the disease. But all that changed on April 19, 1987, when Princess Diana opened the first unit in the UK dedicated to treating people with HIVAIDS. Her televised visit dispelled myths and challenged propaganda. Through the compassionate and courageous act of a gloveless handshake with a patient, she changed people's perceptions of the disease forever.

She brought life to the world as an influencer. She epitomized the impact social media influencers aspire to achieve today. While her royal duties required a constant state of media attention, she was always poised, graceful, and engaging in front of the cameras. Often struggling behind closed doors with loneliness and depression, she used her brand to bring attention to the crises of the world.

Many celebrities and iconic personalities, understand the power of a personal brand. From Oprah Winfrey to Martha Stewart, to former First Lady Michelle Obama, people whose lives are lived in the spotlight are extremely conscious of the image they project. In fact, in many cases, it is that image—their reputation—that helped them rise to such incredible positions of power and influence. Even if you have no desire to be a celebrity, politician, or social media superstar, you'd be wise to recognize what an asset your personal brand can be in terms of your ability to influence others.

YOUR BRAND IS HOW PEOPLE PERCEIVE YOU—WHO YOU ARE, WHAT YOU STAND FOR, AND WHAT YOU VALUE.

To be clear, branding isn't only for celebrities, and it isn't about logos, letterhead, long beards, or the type of clothes you wear. Your brand is the total package. It sums up the impression people have of you. Your brand is how people perceive you—who you are, what you stand for, and what you value. Brand consultant and blogger Jeremiah Gardner notes that this "total package" establishes the relationship that determines how you interact and are received by those around you:

A brand is how we emotionally and intuitively relate to a specific product, organization, or idea. A brand is pointing to something deep inside of us that lives somewhere at the intersection of intention and reception (and the inverse, reception and intention). If we apply this thinking about brand to people, then a 'personal brand' contextually refers to how we relate to a specific person.[61]

Imagine your brand as a building standing at the intersection of your intention and others' perception of it. What does it look like? Did you build it yourself, or did you move into an existing structure? Have you purposefully and carefully designed it? Is it warm and inviting? Or do you have a Sorry, We're Closed sign hanging in the window?

If you haven't thought much about how others see—and more importantly, *remember*—you, it's time!

AUTHENTICITY IS ESSENTIAL

"The most exhausting thing you can do is to be inauthentic."

-ANNE MORROW LINDBERGH

You have quite a bit of control when it comes to how people see you. But as we've discussed in previous chapters, manipulating people's perception of you by presenting a false, "larger than life" image will only backfire. The best, most effective, and profitable way (and in my book, the *only* way) to create a personal brand that sticks, is to share the real you.

Some advertisers may exaggerate products' features to entice people to buy, but branding experts know that inauthenticity can kill a brand. Think of the last time you purchased a brand-name product at the grocery store because its advertising suggested it was fresher, healthier, or tastier than its competitors. Your perception, influenced by marketing, convinced you to try it. If the product lived up to its brand promise, you probably told someone about your happy discovery. But if the product fell short of its promise, I bet you told quite a few people and maybe even ranted about it on Facebook or Twitter. And you may never purchase anything in that brand's family of products again.

Similarly, a personal brand helps you stand out in a crowd. It makes you memorable, demonstrates your value, and gives you an edge over your competition. While those are all admirable goals for your brand, first and foremost your focus should be on establishing an *authentic* brand. When people get what they expect, they aren't disappointed. When others feel that you are genuine in the way you represent yourself, you instantly establish a reputation for being trustworthy. So, keep it real!

Remember, personal branding is not about creating an artificial veneer that hides—or overshadows—your true self, nor is it about changing who you are to make others happy. The goal is for people to know the real you by your reputation. When someone who has read your blog, or listened to your podcast, or followed your posts and tweets, meets you in person for the first time, there should be no disconnect. Rather than meeting a stranger, the congruency between you and your brand should make them feel as if they're meeting an old friend.

AN AUTHENTIC PERSONAL BRAND IS AN IRRESISTIBLE MAGNET THAT WILL ATTRACT PEOPLE AND OPPORTUNITIES TO YOU.

Just as transparency builds trust and connection in your personal relationships, it is an essential element of your personal brand. An authentic personal brand is an irresistible magnet that will attract people and opportunities to you—and because it is aligned with every aspect of your life, it empowers you to become who you truly want to be.

BRAND FROM THE INSIDE OUT

To be authentic is to be true to your personality, spirit, and character. It's the outward manifestation of your core values, as expressed in your lifestyle, relationships, and professional conduct. An authentic brand is built around your own unique identity, a process that requires you to strip away artificial façades or anything that doesn't fit who you want to be.

"The brand begins with the story of you—the experiences that defined you, the lessons you learned, and the ways those lessons shaped your values and beliefs," explains Suzanne Bates in her book, *Discover Your CEO Brand*. "Once you understand the essence of your brand, you will be able to communicate it to the world. It will become a powerful force, creating positive results."[62]

Building an authentic brand begins with identifying the core values that anchor your identity. You may find it helpful to review the core values you identified for yourself at the end of Chapter 2. With your core values in mind, use the following questions to distill your brand down to its essence:

What is your PURPOSE? Why do you exist? What problem are you here to solve? Whom do you want to serve? These are weighty questions, but part of the branding process is using these deep convictions to express who you are.

What is your VISION? What do you want for your life? What do you hope to create, write, build? What are you most excited to accomplish? Whom are you most passionate about helping, teaching, or influencing?

What are you KNOWN FOR? What do people come to you for help with? What are you better at than anyone else? What do you receive the most compliments for?

What is your MISSION? What is the guiding principle that enables you to know if your actions are aligned with your core ambitions, vision, purpose, and aspirations?

The answers to these questions will form the foundation on which your brand is built and bring clarity to your value-adding proposition. Once you've established this footing, resist the temptation to deviate from it. Because you will be pressured to compromise yourself in small ways every day, understanding the importance of authenticity will help you stay true to your brand.

BUILDING A POWERFUL BRAND

"It's important to build a personal brand because it's the only thing you're going to have. Your reputation online, and in the new business world is pretty much the game, so you've got to be a good person. You can't hide anything, and more importantly, you've got to be out there at some level."

-GARY VAYNERCHUK

Gary Vaynerchuk didn't set out to be a multimillionaire. Growing up in New Jersey, he helped his Russian immigrant parents run the family liquor store and began reading *Wine Spectator* magazine when business was slow. Gary was fascinated by its nuanced descriptions of wines, but because he was too young to drink legally, he had to "train his palate backwards." People thought he was crazy when he began sampling the flavors associated with wine, like wood and minerals, but his persistence paid off.

In college, Gary established himself as a local wine expert by tasting every wine that entered the store. Customers came to rely on his no-nonsense advice and discerning palate. Within five years, the store's profits grew from $4 million to $60 million! Gary took his insight to the Internet and launched Wine Library TV, a website committed to educating viewers, debunking myths, and reducing the elitist attitude of the wine industry. Since the site's launch, he has attracted a cultlike following of more than eighty thousand viewers a day.

Gary Vaynerchuk epitomizes the power of a personal brand. While he didn't intend to become famous, the choices he made to leverage his passion and personality set an example for anyone hoping to build a personal brand. Vaynerchuk's story illustrates three components of powerful brands:

They are **distinctive**: Having a brand requires you to have a point of view. That may sound easy, but being distinctive without being odd takes confidence and discernment. Remember that brand building is not the same as image building. Your goal is to bring out your best attributes rather than change yourself to meet others' expectations.

They are **relevant**: Strong brands connect to what others value. Gaining relevance is a process—it starts with questions like, "What do they want?"; "What do they need?"; and "What do they expect?" Just as Gary Vaynerchuk trained his palate in reverse, you can become relevant by "thinking in reverse." As you move out of your own world and into your audience's, you'll be able to connect your skills and abilities to their needs and interests.

Be specific about where you seek relevance. You can't make a connection with everyone, so select your audience strategically. Remember that relevance is reflected in the perceptions others have of you and what you do.

They are **consistent**: Consistency builds trust, a hallmark of a strong brand. Just as consumers expect Coca-Cola to taste the same every time they open a bottle, they depend on you to add value to your work and relationships time and time again.

As you begin building your brand, consider: "How distinctive, relevant, and consistent are you?"

BE DISTINCTIVE

Fashion icon Daphne Guinness knows how to stand out from the crowd. As one of the world's leading collectors of haute couture, her eccentric sense of style often shocks the fashion world. From her trademark black-and-white-streaked hair to her outlandish shoes, Guinness's reputation revolves around her devotion to beauty at any cost.

While many question her singular, lavish focus, Guinness uses her platform to promote the seamstresses, lace makers, and leather workers who create these wearable works of art. In a sea of aspiring fashionistas, her support for these talented artisans sets her apart from the crowd. Daphne Guinness has mastered the art of personal branding and uses her reputation to help others. Her willingness to stand out from the crowd provides insight for anyone hoping to establish a personal brand.

Remember that a brand is personal because *you* have the power to define it. Brand building is not image building or packaging yourself to win a popularity contest; rather, it showcases your unique attributes and demonstrates how you add value to your relationships, workplace, and community. Daphne Guinness identifies herself through fashion, but your personal brand should define who you are and how you make a difference.

> *A BRAND IS PERSONAL BECAUSE ONLY YOU HAVE THE POWER TO DEFINE IT.*

William Arruda and Kirsten Dixson argue that a personal brand is vital to your success: "In today's workplace, creativity has trumped loyalty; individuality has replaced conformity; pro-activity has replaced hierarchy. You don't wait for job assignments—you create them. Those who succeed . . . are aware of their talents and confident enough to use them to stand out and consistently deliver value to their teams."[63] Arruda and Dixson suggest three principles to help you stand out from the crowd:

Principle 1: Stand Out by Standing For Something Special

Instead of waiting for someone to discover you, build your reputation by delivering exceptional service. Entrepreneur and bestselling author Seth Godin explains it this way:

> Most people believe that if they just get their needle sharp enough, it'll magnetically leap out of the haystack and land

wherever it belongs. If they don't get a great job or make a great sale or land a terrific date, it might just be because they don't deserve it. Having met some successful people, I can assure you that they didn't get that way by deserving it...

People are buying only one thing from you: the way the engagement (hiring you, working with you, dating you, using your product or service, learning from you) makes them feel.

So how do you make people feel? Could you make them feel better? More? Could you create the emotions that they're seeking?[64]

Be proactive! Gain a reputation for your unique attributes or for the exceptional service you provide.

Principle 2: Be Your Own Boss

Instead of waiting for someone to discover you, take ownership for your success. Even if you can't control the circumstances, you can control your personal brand. Arruda and Dixson remind readers that talent, not titles, brings security: "Your skills and unique personal attributes don't disappear if your company's stock price plummets. Your future doesn't unravel if an executive who powerfully supported your advancement leaves the company. Your personal assets are yours, and no one can take them away from you."[65] Take responsibility for your career by using your assets to your advantage. Let your brand, rather than your circumstances, open doors for you.

Principle 3: Focus on the Ramp, Not the Ladder

Most people think of their career as a ladder, with progressive milestones or advancements along the way. They work hard and put forth a burst of energy to get a promotion or secure their position.

However, in today's economy, it's more fruitful to regard your career as a steady walk up a ramp rather than a jump up the ladder. When you ascend a ramp, you are in perpetual motion and build momentum as you climb. Instead of waiting for outside forces to trigger your advancement, begin advancing now by developing a network of contacts, updating your résumé, and pursuing opportunities that showcase your strengths. When you shift your mindset to build your brand and career every day, you will make steady progress to the top.

How will you stand out from the crowd? Building your brand by taking ownership for your career is a powerful way to ensure your success.

BE RELEVANT

Think of the last time you met someone who only talked about him- or herself. It may have been a friend from high school, who recapped the last twenty years of her life but never asked how you were doing. Or maybe it was an acquaintance at a networking meeting who droned on about his latest project without inquiring what you do for a living. Anyone who has spent time with a self-focused person knows the frustration of a one-sided exchange.

As you hone your brand, remember that a brand, though personal, is not exclusively about you. Defining your brand is about moving beyond "I, me, and mine" to consider how you can add value to your relationships. In their book *Be Your Own Brand*, authors David McNally and Karl Speak remind us that, "Strong personal brands thrive in finding ways to contribute and make a positive difference for others."[66]

Developing an others-focused brand begins with understanding your audience's needs. Whether you are a teacher connecting with your students' parents or a project manager supervising a team of engineers, knowing your clientele will empower you to match your unique abilities to a specific situation. In the process, you'll become known as someone who listens, connects, and cares.

So instead of focusing on your own goals, focus on building mutually beneficial, value-adding, purpose-driven, achievement-oriented, collaborative relationships. The next time you have a professional networking opportunity, try shifting your perspective from "What's in it for me?" to "How can we help each other?" It's a subtle change that produces dramatic results. When people realize that you're interested in their success, you'll gain a reputation as someone who is generous, supportive, and resourceful.

Finally, make trust the foundation of your brand. "When you make a discernible difference in the life of another, you make a lasting impression and your brand receives credit—a deposit in the 'trust bank,'" explain McNally and Speak. "Every meaningful impression adds more 'credits' that build toward the establishment of a trusting relationship."[67]

Although it may seem counterintuitive, focusing on others is one of the best ways to establish your own brand. Identifying their needs, pursuing mutually beneficial relationships, and building a foundation of trust will enhance your reputation.

BE CONSISTENT

McDonald's golden arches are one of the most recognizable symbols in the world. Every day, nearly sixty-nine million people stop in for a bite to eat at one of the thirty-four thousand locations worldwide.[68] Did that fame come from serving the best food? Or delivering it faster than others? Sorry, no. There are plenty of places that serve a better burger, and even a few who can do it faster. But no restaurant chain serves *more* burgers.

So why do people return again and again to this fast-food giant? In a word, *consistency*. If you visit a McDonald's in any of the 118 countries where the franchise operates, the burgers, fries, and chicken nuggets will taste almost exactly the same. Your order will be delivered on a tray or in a bag and handed across a familiar-looking counter by someone wearing clothing you recognize. That consistent, quick delivery of familiar flavors in a no-surprise atmosphere makes McDonald's a sure bet. Even if the food isn't great, at least you know you'll get what you expect.

Consistency is what people want from you, too. Not that you have to wear the same outfit every day, or have a catch phrase like "Do you want fries with that?" You don't even have to stay in the same career your whole life. A desire to be consistent doesn't preclude growth or change. McDonald's has certainly seen plenty of growth and change—remodeling locations and adding chicken sandwiches and salads to the menu, for example. But every change is in line with the organization's family-friendly food brand.

In terms of your personal brand, being consistent requires you to be who you are—all the time. Your family life, lifestyle, image, words, hobbies, online presence— everything about you should match up with your values. When a friend learns something new about you, their first response shouldn't be, "I never would have expected that from you!" Rather, even if your passion for, say, skydiving surprises people, they should be able to say, "Yes, that fits with what I know about you."

CONSISTENCY IS WHAT PEOPLE WANT FROM YOU.

The same principle applies equally to your career. "You cannot separate business life from the rest of your life when it comes to building a brand,"[69] writes Suzanne Bates in *Discover Your CEO Brand*. To help your network, clients, and potential clients understand and remember your brand *the way you want them to*, your actions, associations, and attitudes must be consistent with your core values.

You have a great deal of control over the way the world receives and remembers you. It starts with knowing who you are and being true to your core values. "Leaders have a brand based on authentic values they use to influence others. [Your] brand is the core of who you are as a leader and how you are perceived," Bates explains. When you share who you are—distinctively, relevantly, and consistently—you build a personal brand that others trust. And trust is the key to increasing your capacity to influence others. In the next chapter, we'll focus on additional ways to boost your credibility so as to cement your trustworthiness in others' minds.

 WINNING ACTION: *DEFINE YOUR BRAND*

To better understand the perception others have of you, and that you have of yourself, answer the following questions using one-word or one-phrase answers:

What do you say about yourself?
- What's the strongest personality trait that you project to others?
- What value or moral principle do others associate with you?
- For what skill, talent, or ability are you best known?
- Describe your personal style.

What do others say about you? (Ask a friend, co-worker, or loved one to help.)
- What do you see as a dominant characteristic of my personality?
- When you think of me, what value or moral principle comes to mind?
- What is my most prominent skill, talent, or ability?
- How would you describe me to someone who has never met me?

What effect do you have on others?
- How do acquaintances most commonly introduce you to someone you've never met before?

- What topics most frequently come up in your conversations?
- When you meet people for the first time, they often develop a "gut feeling" about you. On a scale of 1 to 10, how strong is their first impression of you? (1 = weak, 10 = strong)

(Re)Shape Your Brand

- Ask yourself: "Am I happy with these perceptions?"
- Make a pros/cons list that describes how these perceptions support or hinder the brand you are creating.

As you conclude this chapter, spend a few moments considering this quote from marketer Seth Godin:

> Every action, every word, every element of your appearance and your projected personality is a choice: leave it to chance and hope that people will understand the message you really want to communicate, or take control of the process and send the message you intend to send.[70]

Consider whether these impressions help you achieve your goals. If they don't reflect the brand by which you want to be known, it's up to you to become the person you want others to see.*

---

* For a deeper dive into personal branding, read my book *Irresistible*.

Chapter 9

CULTIVATE
WINNING CREDIBILITY

"Trust is the glue of life. It's the most essential ingredient in effective communication. It's the foundational principle that holds all relationships."

-STEPHEN R. COVEY

In 2012, America's trust that the media reported news "fully, accurately, and fairly" hit an all-time low.[71]

Security breaches at Target and Neiman Marcus during the 2013 holiday shopping season rattled consumer confidence when as many as 110 million people's personal data was exposed.[72] Gallup polls indicate declining levels of trust in respect to federal government's executive, legislative, and judicial branches,[73] and an increasing sense of pessimism toward the economy.[74]

Americans don't even trust the "American people" to make sound political judgments.[75]

Clearly, Americans have trust issues. And perhaps, for good reason. The lack of trust that seems to permeate the American psyche stems from a *lack of trustworthiness*. Almost every minute of network news is devoted to highlighting the ways people cheat, lie to, steal from, and hurt their fellow man. Even if we don't implicitly trust the media, it's hard to ignore the sheer quantity of negative reports.

But there is good news for you amid all of this distrust. If you can develop a reputation of one who is credible, you will stand out like a light piercing through the darkness. The brighter you shine, the more people's attention you will attract. So, the question is, are you credible? Can others trust you?

WHAT DOES IT MEAN TO BE CREDIBLE?

Credibility refers to the believability of an individual's or an organization's reputation. When people view you as credible, it means that they believe you are real and true, that you will fulfill your promises, and that you aren't just out for yourself.

I am reminded of a story I heard about an old miser who thought he was very clever. As happened, he lost his purse containing a hundred pieces of gold. So he went to the town crier and asked him to announce a reward of ten gold coins to the one who found it. After a few days, a farmer came to him with the purse. He had found it lying on the ground. The miser counted the money and found the purse contained a hundred pieces of gold. He thanked the farmer for the pains he had taken.

But the farmer wanted the reward as announced. The miser told the farmer he must have already taken the reward because originally there had been one hundred and ten coins in the purse. The farmer now understood how clever the miser was. He went to the judge to state his case. The judge sent for the miser and after hearing his explanation, understood that the miser was a trickster. The judge said that the purse found by the farmer contained only one hundred gold coins, so it must not belong to the miser. He ruled in favor of the farmer keeping the purse he had found.[76]

Compromising your credibility can be costly.

While in the previous chapter we discussed building a personal brand that reflects your identity and core values, you must also build your credibility. You must intentionally craft your reputation and image so as to shape people's perceptions of you. That's good because branding is an important tool that can help you increase your capacity to influence others. But personal branding isn't a gimmick that you can employ to secure your place in people's hearts and minds. Even if you are able to make a positive impression, you must continue, day in and day out, to uphold your reputation. Credibility is how you do that. It is your strategy for maintaining and strengthening both your brand and your influence. It's how you get people to "know, like, and trust" you on a long-term basis.

THREE (MORE) KEYS TO CULTIVATING CREDIBILITY

Throughout this book, I've repeated words like *integrity*, *authenticity*, *core values*, *transparency*, and *consistency*. All of these concepts are essential to establishing credibility. Additionally, *conviction*, *compassion*, and *competence* can help you shine brighter in people's memory, cementing you in their minds as a person they can trust as a friend and as a leader.

CONVICTION

When you believe in your dream, your purpose,

> YOUR UNSHAKABLE BELIEF INSPIRES PEOPLE TO BELIEVE IN YOU AND YOUR VISION.

your goal, and *yourself*, you radiate a sense of confidence that others notice. Even if they don't "get" your goal or dream, they can't deny your commitment to achieving it.

Your unshakable belief inspires people to believe in you and your vision. And as we'll discuss further in the next section, your conviction also inspires people to believe in their ability to transform *their* lives. Your belief is critical. As John Maxwell writes in *Put Your Dream to the Test*, "Convincing others of the significance of your dream can happen only if you are convinced of the significance of your dream."[77]

Developing conviction begins with knowing who you are and what your core values are, and then anchoring your goals to those truths about yourself. One way to strengthen your conviction or belief in your goal is to use daily declarations. These positive, focused statements should be spoken aloud to affirm your beliefs and desires to yourself—and how they make you feel will provide an indicator of whether you truly believe them.

Take a moment to think about a goal or desire you have for your life. First, put it to the test by asking:

- Is this my goal, or is it something that another person or society at large has told me I "should" want?
- Is this goal rooted in my core values? In other words, is it in alignment with my true identity and sense of self?

If you can honestly answer that your goal is *your* goal—and that it aligns with what you know to be true about yourself, great! Now write a declaration to reinforce your belief in yourself and in your goal. Make your declaration positive, in the present, and purposeful. Below are a few declarations I've used in the past. Feel free to use them or to revise them to fit your own unique situation and dreams.

- Instead of striving to do everything, I will focus on doing what matters most to me.
- I possess everything I need within myself to go after my goals!
- Whoever can be trusted with very little can also be trusted with much. I am trustworthy.
- Good intentions are not good enough! I commit to turning my ideas into action.

Speaking declarations aloud daily helps instill the conviction you need to inspire others to trust and believe in you. Ultimately, however, your conviction will be made evident not by the words you speak, but by the actions you take. You gain credibility when your conviction empowers you to "walk the talk."

COMPASSION

"People don't care how much you know until they know how much you care."

-JOHN C. MAXWELL

Daniel Goleman, author of the groundbreaking book *Emotional Intelligence*, told this story of compassion he personally experienced in a subway station:

> At the end of the day on a Friday, I was going down the subway; it was rush hour. Thousands of people were streaming down the stairs, and all of a sudden, I noticed that there was a man, slumped to the side, shirtless, and not moving. And people were just stepping over him, hundreds and hundreds of people. I found myself stopping to find out what was wrong. The moment I stopped, half a dozen other people stopped. We found out he was Hispanic, he didn't speak any English, and he had no money. He had wandered the streets for days, starving, and fainted from hunger. Immediately someone went to get orange juice and someone ran to get a hot dog. The guy was back on his feet quickly. All it took was that simple act of noticing.[78]

As heartwarming as this story is, it leaves me wondering, "Why did hundreds of people walk past the suffering man?"

We each encounter people in need every day. It might be a co-worker battling a chronic illness, a widowed neighbor dealing with grief, or a harried mother struggling to manage her children in the checkout line at the grocery store. You may not be able to resolve each person's problem, but simple acts of compassion can ease their pain.

COMPASSION IS EMPATHY IN ACTION.

Compassion is empathy in action. It's about seeing a person's need and responding in practical ways. Compassion has the power to transform lives and communities. When you act with compassion, the people around you recognize that you care about others. They see that you're not just in this life for yourself, but to empower and encourage others.

Simple acts of compassion can make such a difference. So, why don't we show kindness more often? Ask yourself if any of the following issues keep you from responding compassionately:

Self-absorption. This happens when your focus is directed toward yourself. Many people are so absorbed by their own interests that they never even notice another person's needs. Showing compassion can seem inconvenient or costly; you might get dirty or give up a small luxury to provide for someone's immediate need.

An overloaded schedule. When you fill every moment of the day, it's a hassle to deviate from your plans. You may be so busy rushing to the next appointment that you simply don't notice the people you pass along the way.

Daniel Goleman said that the incident in the subway "shook him out of his urban trance,"[79] a common experience for many commuters. If your typical response is, "I don't have time for this," you may lack space in your schedule to act compassionately.

Isolation. Have you ever changed lanes at an intersection to avoid making eye contact with a homeless man, or avoided discussing a painful subject with a friend because you didn't know what to say? By avoiding a situation, you can escape painful realities, but this isolation can also create judgmental stereotypes. Author Anne McCaffrey cautioned: "Make no judgments where you have no compassion."[80] When you don't understand a person's experience, it's easy to blame them for their predicament.

Intimidation. Fear can keep you from responding compassionately. Maybe you encounter a situation that you've never experienced before and you don't know what to do or say. Fear of the unknown causes us to withdraw, removing ourselves from situations where we could show compassion. Here's how one woman shared about how she dealt with these fears:

> I remember the summer I worked in urban Los Angeles. Friends and I committed to serve a weekly breakfast to the homeless people in our neighborhood. The first day we served, I was terrified! I had never made conversation with a homeless person before and didn't know what to say. I spent the morning in the kitchen brewing coffee and preparing doughnuts, but was too scared to do any more. Each week I was a little braver and by the end of the summer, I looked forward to interacting with the men and women we served.

When a person is suffering, it's natural to be at a loss for words. A simple, caring response such as, "I don't know what to say, but I want to support you in this experience," can help you connect with a person in pain.

It takes time *and* practice to learn how to act compassionately, so don't let your initial awkwardness hold you back! Let compassion flow through you to meet your community's deepest needs.

> "By compassion we make others' misery our own,
> and so, by relieving them, we relieve ourselves also."
> -SIR THOMAS BROWNE

What keeps you from responding compassionately? Of the issues described above, which connects with you? How can you grow in this area?

Take a few moments to brainstorm a list of needs in:

- Your neighborhood
- Your church
- Your city

How can you use your gifts, time, money, experience, and/or energy to meet these needs?

COMPETENCE

"No work is insignificant. All labor that uplifts humanity has dignity and importance and should be undertaken with painstaking excellence."

-MARTIN LUTHER KING JR.

To be impeccable is to be faultless or irreproachable. Impeccability implies excellence. Obviously, no one on earth is perfect. We all have faults and weaknesses. So I want to be clear in stating that impeccability is not about perfectionism or creating a rule-based or legalistic standard for achievement. Rather, for our purposes, impeccability is about committing to continual personal growth and to giving life your very best. Two ways to ensure your impeccability are to inspect what you expect of yourself, and to intentionally boost your competence.

Inspect what you expect. Determine to set a standard of personal excellence for your relationships, your health, your finances, and your work. What are your non-negotiables for these core areas? For example, a standard of excellence that can be applied to every area is honesty. A commitment to honesty in your relationships eliminates lies, infidelity, and other relationship-risking behaviors. Honesty in regard to your health could mean a commitment to not trying to fool yourself and count the walk to the parking lot as exercise or ice cream as a dairy serving, or trying to convince yourself that you don't have to quit smoking. Honesty in your finances could mean that you refuse to fudge on your taxes by taking extra deductions.

Honesty in regard to work should mean that you keep your promises and deliver top-quality products on time.

Once you've identified your non-negotiables, conduct periodic evaluations. Relax. I'm not asking you to do extra paperwork, although you may want to make notes in your journal. Simply look back on your day and ask yourself, "Did I live up to my expectations of excellence today?" If the answer is, "I could have done better," determine where you need to make improvements and/or amends.

With the busyness of life, it's very easy to set goals and then zip from one activity to the next and forget all about them. Your personal standards are **COMMIT TO INSPECTING WHAT YOU EXPECT DAILY.** too important to your integrity and identity to let them slip under the radar. Commit to inspecting what you expect daily.

Boost your competence. Credibility isn't about academic knowledge, but it is about how others see you applying what you know. If people feel you are competent or capable of performing a particular task, they will reach out to you for advice or support. Your competence makes others confident in their decision to work with and trust you.

If you want to be impeccable in the way you live and work, be intentional about adding to your knowledge and raising your skill level. Doing so will improve not only your ability to perform, but your confidence (and others' confidence in you), as well.

Identify the areas of your life (particularly in relation to your work) that need improvement and use the following tactics to boost your competence:

- Read books (not just blogs and social media posts).
- Take a course.
- Complete your degree, or earn another one.
- Practice, practice, practice.
- Hire a coach or trainer.

HOW TO REBUILD BROKEN TRUST

"When you stumble, nothing beats being humble."

-HARVEY MACKAY

No one is perfect. From the working mom who misses her child's school play, to the spouse who "fooled around" with a co-worker, to a doctor who misdiagnosed a patient, or a leader whose actions sought personal gain rather than the good of his/her followers, everyone has made mistakes. And all of us will slip up again (and again). Our humanity makes us fallible.

Thankfully, we each have a conscience that alerts us to our moral, ethical, and relational failings. When you feel that twinge in your gut or a sadness in your heart, pay attention. It could very well be your conscience warning you to stop and turn toward what you know to be right. Like an internal compass, your conscience will point you back to the way you *should* be going—the way that aligns with your core values and the truth of who you are.

Don't disregard that voice or the people who care enough to call you out on bad behavior. Listen and take action to repair the breach of trust. It may be embarrassing to admit your mistake, but I promise, it's unlikely to be fatal. On the other hand, ignoring or denying your faults—or worse, blaming others for them—will ultimately lead to ruin.

When your conscience sounds off warning bells, here are five steps you can take to begin to repair your damaged credibility:

1. **Be Humble.** "Pride leads to disgrace, but with humility comes wisdom," (Proverbs 11:2 nlt). Those words are as true today as they were when King Solomon wrote them almost three thousand years ago. Pride keeps us from seeing our own faults, so we sink deeper into them. Humility opens our eyes and hearts to the reality that we have the potential to

make mistakes. Practice humility. Be humble enough to listen to your conscience and to those who point out your error.

2. **Admit Your Mistake.** Until you admit a mistake, it's difficult to do anything about it. Now, I'm not saying you need to hold a full-court press conference. At a minimum, admit your guilt to yourself. Owning your faults or failures is a step toward correcting them. Sometimes—many times, in fact—it won't be enough to simply recognize your fault, because other people are almost always affected by your behavior. Find those people and tell them, "I was wrong."

    Taking ownership of your behavior requires that you refuse to make excuses or blame others—ever. The reality is that external circumstances could have triggered an action or reaction. But remember, each person is responsible for their own behavior. Period. So when you confess your mistake, resist the urge to shift blame. Take etiquette expert Barbara Pachter's advice: "Don't make excuses for your behavior if you're wrong. 'Well, you see, I haven't been sleeping well and my brother is in the hospital and the holidays are coming up...' You're going to sound like a jerk if you make excuses."[81]

3. **Apologize.** Saying "I was wrong," is an excellent start. But don't stop there. When spoken sincerely, the words, "I'm sorry," carry tremendous healing powers. In her book, *The Power of Apology*, Beverly Engel explains that saying "I'm sorry," is only a matter of politeness or etiquette: "It is also a way of acknowledging an act that can't go unnoticed without compromising the relationship. Apology has the ability to disarm the anger of others, to prevent future misunderstandings, and to bridge the distances between people," she writes. "In some instances, it even has the ability to rehabilitate an indi-

vidual, resolve conflicts, and restore social harmony."[82] That's a lot of power packed into two simple words!

When you admit your fault and say, "I'm sorry," you ultimately empower the other person to forgive you.

4. **Make Amends.** Follow your apology with real effort to right the wrong. You may even ask the person or people you've hurt, "What can I do to make things right?" While you can't change the past, you can learn from your mistakes and avoid making them again. If you owe a debt, repay it in full. If you broke or lost something, replace it. If you're the mother who missed the spring concert, spend extra time with your child and make certain not to miss the next important event in his or her life. Sometimes no gift or payment will be appropriate. In those cases, the best thing you can do is focus on rebuilding your reputation.

5. **Rebuild Your Reputation.** In *The Mackay MBA of Selling in the Real World*, author and entrepreneur Harvey Mackay recounts the story of Michael Milken, who was nicknamed the "Junk Bond King" and indicted for insider trading, racketeering, and securities fraud in 1989. He was sentenced to ten years in prison and fined $600 million. He served twenty-two months before being released for good behavior. A week later, Milken was diagnosed with prostate cancer and told he had twelve to eighteen months to live.[83] From that moment, Milken's life took a dramatic turn. He radically changed his diet and lifestyle. "He beat the disease, but Milken didn't stop there," Mackay writes.

Mike Milken reorganized the war on cancer. He founded the Prostate Cancer Foundation. It's the world's biggest source of prostate cancer research funding. His management savvy has accelerated the pace of prostate cancer research. Experts say he's a force in cutting cancer fatalities. *Fortune* magazine put him on its cover and dubbed him "The Man Who Changed Medicine."[84]

Milken didn't want to be remembered for his massive and public failings, so he set a course to rebuild an honorable reputation.

Your mistakes may never be as financially costly or as publicly discussed as someone like Milken. But you can apply the same principle of rebuilding your reputation with your child, your spouse, your clients, your company, or your community. Begin by using the keys to cultivating credibility: honesty, compassion, and impeccability. Hold yourself accountable to others by living transparently. Use your core values as beacons to help you stay on course to becoming the best version of yourself.

> *HOLD YOURSELF ACCOUNTABLE TO OTHERS BY LIVING TRANSPARENTLY.*

In the final section of *Unstoppable: Compete with Yourself and Win*, we will look at how all of these life-transforming mindsets, skills, habits, and practices work together to shape you into a strong and worthy leader.

WINNING ACTION: *ARE YOU CREDIBLE?*

Rank yourself on a scale of 1 to 10 for each of the following questions.
   1 = never, 10 = always.

____ I tell the truth.

____ I can be trusted to keep a secret.

____ I listen when others talk.

____ I notice other people's needs.

____ I am always on time or early to meetings and events.

____ I am confident in my ability to perform my job.

____ My family members and friends know they can count on me to be available to them physically and emotionally.

____ I admit when I am wrong.

____ I finish what I start.

____ I keep my promises.

Tally your score.

The closer your total is to 100, the more people perceive you as credible.

SECTION FOUR
THE WINNER'S CIRCLE

"There's an inner power that makes winners or losers. The winners are the ones who really listen to the truth of their hearts."

-SYLVESTER STALLONE

With this final section of *Unstoppable: Compete with Yourself and Win*, I hope to inspire you to move beyond living authentically to *leading* authentically.

Winning is about so much more than you and your desires and dreams. Certainly, these are important. But your true greatness is released when you embrace the fact that your purpose isn't to serve yourself, but to empower others to improve the world. That's real transformation; that's real leadership. And that's the focus of this fourth and final section.

I realize you may not think of yourself as a leader—yet. Sure, you know by now that your attitude and actions influence others. But do you really *lead* others? I believe you do—that we all do in our unique way. To some extent, you are already a leader in your home, your community, your workplace, and your social groups. With the first chapter in this section, "Leaders Who Win," I implore you to become *intentional* with your leadership. It's important to know whom you are leading and how you can become a more effective and empowering leader.

The next chapter, "Serve to Win," offers a better way to lead: *through service*. If your idea of a leader is the person who barks directions from the sidelines, this chapter will challenge you to get your hands dirty. Servant-leadership is a time-honored concept that is making an impressive difference in today's transparent world. And it's a philosophy you can use to make your mark...which leads us to the final chapter in this section, "Leave a Winning Legacy."

Legacy is a big, often misunderstood word that is frequently tossed around without much thought. More than the money and material goods you leave behind, your legacy—what people remember about how you helped them—can influence the way people live long after you've stepped out of their lives. In this chapter, you'll learn how to use all the skills, strategies, and philosophies we've discussed in *Unstoppable* to leave a legacy that inspires people for generations to come. We'll look more specifically at purpose, so you can define in the grander scale of life how to use your identity, values, and unique strengths and gifts to make an unstoppable impact on the world.

USE YOUR IDENTITY, VALUES, AND STRENGTHS TO MAKE AN UNSTOPPABLE IMPACT ON THE WORLD.

You have only one lifetime with which to make your mark. The people you lead, the manner in which you lead them, and the legacy you create for them will determine the ultimate impact of your life. If you want to win, you've got to make your life count.

Chapter 10

LEADERS WHO WIN

"Leadership is action, not position."

-PETER DRUCKER

Do you see yourself as a leader?

If you don't have a lofty business title or hold a political office, you may not consider yourself a leader. You may think you're "just" a parent, employee, or retiree with no "real" power.

Think again. As John Maxwell says, "Everyone is a leader because everyone influences someone."

In Chapter 7, we discussed the truth that regardless of your title, position, authority, or resources, you have the potential to influence others. If influence is your ability to affect the behavior of another person without forcing them into action, leadership goes one step further in that it is both intentional and goal oriented. The goal of *empowered leadership* is to change the world by equipping and encouraging people to become their best, most authentic selves. Because if you, *as just one person*, can change the world by becoming your best self, consider the possibilities when your circle of influence follows suit.

EVERYONE IS A LEADER—EVEN YOU!

"The most dangerous leadership myth is that leaders are born— that there is a genetic factor to leadership. This myth asserts that people simply either have certain charismatic qualities or not. That's nonsense; in fact, the opposite is true. Leaders are made rather than born."

-WARREN BENNIS

I know you've heard the term *born leader*. Right now, this instant, I want you to recognize the fallacy of that phrase. We are born as babies, with no ability to care for ourselves—much less lead others.

IF YOU CAN CHANGE THE WORLD BY BECOMING YOUR BEST SELF, CONSIDER THE POSSIBILITIES WHEN YOUR CIRCLE OF INFLUENCE FOLLOWS SUIT.

Babies are not leaders, but they *do* have influence. If you're a parent, you remember all the sleepless nights spent walking with, singing to, or rocking your child. And do you recall the lengths you went to find your child's favorite pacifier, blanket, or stuffed animal? Yes, our little ones influenced our behavior and even our attitudes. Babies can draw out a smile from even the most serious adults. Do a quick YouTube search for "laughing baby," and you'll find more than one million video clips of sweet, genuine, uninhibited laughter. Watch one, and your mood will lift in a matter of seconds. You don't even *know* that baby, and still his or her laughter will cause you to feel happier and perhaps even to share your happiness with another person. A baby's ability to affect your behavior and even your mood is influence, but it isn't leadership.

Leadership is purpose-driven influence. We've seen plenty of examples in the media of leaders whose purposes were self-centered and self-rewarding. Those leaders are driven by the desire for personal gain, wealth, or position. They direct people's actions and manipulate outcomes that serve themselves with no thought of how their selfishness damages their relationships, others' well-being, or even the national economy.

In contrast, empowered, transformational leaders are others-focused. They are concerned not only for themselves, but also for the well-being and the improvement of the people around them—and even the world at large.

When I think of people who are making a purposeful, positive impact, I think of people like Melinda Gates. As a vocal gender equity advocate, she has been instrumental in working to improve women's health and welfare around the world. Through the foundation she leads, populations with limited resources are given access to the services and information they need to improve their lives. That's one end of the leadership spectrum. On the other end is a man named Mr. Barnes, who lived in my birth country of Bermuda. Every morning, Mr. Barnes awoke, dressed, and went down to stand on the side of the road to wave to motorists journeying to work in rush-hour traffic. Rain, wind, or shine, for four hours he waved and smiled, exclaiming, "I love you! Have a nice day!" To some, this may seem eccentric or insignificant. To others, his words came at just the right moment.

LEADERSHIP IS PURPOSE-DRIVEN INFLUENCE.

Through the years, Mr. Barnes created positive changes in countless lives. Many people have testified, "Mr. Barnes, you turned my day around. You helped me see a different perspective. You helped me change my outlook on life."

What do Bill and Melinda Gates and Mr. Barnes have in common? Each of them followed an inner passion—an inner drive to see how they might make the world a little different, a little better. That's what I call leading from the inside out, and that is the most effective, and most authentic, kind of leadership.

CHARACTERISTICS OF AN EMPOWERED LEADER

"People today are desperate for leaders, but they want to be influenced only by individuals they can trust, persons of good character."

-JOHN MAXWELL AND JIM DORNAN

When people use the term *born leader*, they're often referring to a person's natural proclivity for communication or his/her ability to connect with or relate to people because of their persuasive and charismatic personality. In Chapter 4, we discussed the truth that all individuals are uniquely wired and gifted with particular strengths and attributes. It's true that people with an Influencer personality type are naturally outgoing. While these "high Is" may have an easier time of talking with people, their personality does not automatically make them good leaders. Nor does the quiet nature of someone who is predominately driven by a Steady or Compliant personality preclude them from leading well. In fact, in her book *Quiet: The Power of Introverts in a World That Can't Stop Talking*, Susan Cain notes that as a society, we often overestimate how outgoing leaders need to be. The truth is, quiet and self-reflective people can be strong leaders. "Because of their inclination to listen to others and lack of interest in dominating social situations, introverts are more likely to hear and implement suggestions. Having benefited from the talents of their followers, they are then likely to motivate them to be even more proactive."[85] Certainly, your natural personality shapes the way you express yourself as a leader, but there is no "born leader" personality type.

Leadership isn't a gift that's bestowed on a select few. It is a skill that is developed over time. We become leaders through a journey toward personal, spiritual, and relational maturity. Your leadership is shaped by your experiences, your insight, and your strength of character. We become leaders the moment we take responsibility for the impact our lives have on others. Everyone, *especially you*, can be a winning leader. I say *"especially you"* because, as proven by your choice to read this book, you are among the wise, who realize the importance of intentional personal development. And if you'll apply the life-transforming mindsets, habits, and practices of authenticity, integrity, and impeccability to your leadership development, as well, you will most definitely make a difference in this world.

HAVE A STRONG SENSE OF IDENTITY

To move forward with this focus on becoming an empowered leader, we must first go back to the beginning—to your very identity. Bob Rosen, founder of Healthy Companies International and author of *Grounded: How Leaders Stay Rooted in an Uncertain World*, explains that establishing your identity must come first: "Quality leadership stems not from what a person does but who that person is inside himself. Meaningful actions can take place only after a person has looked deep inside himself and knows what he's all about."[86]

A strong sense of identity is like a well-established root system. The seasons may bring changes and even harsh conditions, but the tree whose roots run deep is able to withstand external challenges. So it is with your identity. Establishing a firm understanding of who you are, your purpose, and your core values will help you maintain a clear perspective as you face new and greater leadership challenges. That's good for you as well as for those whom you lead.

"With healthy roots, leaders not only are more fulfilled and reach their potential but have an effect on other individuals and vast organizations," Rosen writes. "They motivate people around them to perform at their best and they inspire companies and even the communities in which they operate to benefit the greater good. Along the way and not incidentally, their healthy leadership has been shown to produce tangible results in a company's operations and bottom line."[87]

Unfortunately, the first thing many people unintentionally do when they venture into a leadership role is to lose themselves in the hoopla of titles and power. The promise of profit, the pressure to accomplish more, and the powerful desire to impress or please people can tempt people to abandon their true identity. They try to be all things to all people and forget who they are. Ultimately, this loss of identity disappoints their followers and, worse, themselves.

EMPOWERED LEADERSHIP REQUIRES AUTHENTICITY.

Empowered leadership requires authenticity. Here are a few ways to ensure your root system—your true identity—remains intact.

- **Nourish yourself.** Take care of yourself from the inside out. If you are worn out, stressed out, or burned out, you're at greater risk of making inauthentic choices, either to please people or in hopes of making a problem go away.

  Start with the basics: Get the rest and nutrition your body needs to perform at optimum levels. Then, feed your mind daily with positive, inspirational messages that remind you of your core values and your commitment to your purpose.

- **Protect yourself from erosion.** Meet regularly with a mentor or adviser who knows the real you. Ideally, this trusted individual has been in your life for a while. He or she may be able to recognize any concerning shifts in your attitude and/ or behavior before you are able to see them yourself.

- **Stay connected to your core.** In *Grounded*, Rosen suggests the following questions for self-reflection. Answering them will help you remember and stay true to who you are and what you value most. And if you're honest with your responses, these questions will help you recognize the circumstances in which you may be risking your authenticity.

  → "What are the core values that transcend both my personal and work life?"
  → "When I go home at night, what thoughts about the day give me the most satisfaction?"
  → "What gets me excited and eager during the day?"
  → "Are there certain people or situations that I consistently avoid?"
  → "What is my typical reaction when I receive feedback about myself from others?"
  → "Do I quickly identify counterproductive thoughts or self-talk?"

ACT WITH INTEGRITY

Identity = Knowing **who you are.**

Integrity = Being **who you are.**

Remember the *Merriam-Webster* definition of *integrity*: "the quality or state of being **complete** or **undivided**."

Just as it is important to your mental and emotional well-being to behave in a manner that is congruent with your identity, integrity is equally essential to your ability to lead. To make a lasting impact, your entire life must be integrated—whole and without discrepancies between your identity and your words and actions.

The questions listed above will help you remember your identity. Acting with integrity requires that you address your weak spots—places in your life where you are saying one thing and doing another. Use your answers to these follow-up questions to bring your life into alignment.

- What areas of your personal or work life are not in alignment with your core values? How does this incongruence affect your team? What do you need to do, give up, or change to ensure that your core values are not violated?

- How can you spend more of your day doing what you love? Can you delegate tasks that don't use your strengths or fit your personality style? What one thing could you change that would change everything—for yourself and for those you lead?

- If you are consistently avoiding certain people or situations, why is that? What needs to change? Do these relationships need to be repaired? Or, perhaps, should the relationship be ended? Create a plan today for resolving this situation.

- How will you speak to yourself going forward? Write a declaration that reminds you of who you are and what you stand for. When you feel tempted to deviate from what you know to be true about you, repeat your declaration aloud.

Your example leads the way for your followers. By making complete integrity a priority, you empower your family members, friends, and co-workers to hold true to their values.

CONTINUALLY BUILD CREDIBILITY

"Integrity, trust, and credibility are the foundations of leadership. Leaders stand up for what they believe in. Leaders keep their promises."
—BRIAN TRACY AND PETER CHEE

As you learned in the previous chapter, credibility requires continual effort. It isn't something you do for a while and then stop when you have "enough." Especially in today's interconnected and transparent world, there is no fooling people. That's why it is so important to know your true identity and core values—so you don't have to put on an act.

Brad Lomenick, author of *The Catalyst Leader*, explains, "I've learned that leaders are defined by their inner strengths and convictions, not the outer portrayal of who they are. Your character will determine your level of leadership and even your legacy. Reputation can't be delegated.... It takes a lifetime to build, but only a few seconds to lose."[88]

> CHARACTER IS THE FOUNDATION UPON WHICH YOUR CREDIBILITY AS A LEADER IS BUILT.

Character is the foundation upon which your credibility as a leader is built. You've already done the work of defining who you are and what you stand for. And with an awareness of the importance of integrity, you are well on your way to building a solid reputation. Additionally, the practices that follow will further strengthen the trust others have in you.

Keep your cool. Leadership can put you in frustrating, difficult, or even scary situations. As an empowered leader, you must refuse to allow the emotions of fear or anger to usurp your personal power.

I'm sure you've heard of bosses whom people avoided or lied to for fear of their reaction to problems. You may have even been in a workplace where you felt as if you had to "walk on eggshells." Rants, cursing, or violent displays of emotion have no place in the life of a leader who hopes to empower and transform others. Outbursts demolish credibility.

In contrast, when your followers know that you can retain control of your emotions during stressful circumstances, they are more likely to trust you and support your efforts—even in challenging times.

Check your calendar. In *Leadership Sustainability*, Dave Ulrich and Norm Smallwood explain that hypocrisy (the enemy of credibility) happens when a leader's stated priorities don't match up with their actions. Your followers (which may include your children, spouse, team members at work, and/or the people in your community) constantly compare your actions to your words.

If left unchecked, busyness can work against leaders and sabotage their credibility. "Leaders always have a mirror in which to view themselves, a mirror that will replace hypocrisy with credibility: The calendar. A calendar reflects what we do and not what we say, and it offers an honest look at our priorities, both past and future," write Ulrich and Smallwood. Do an end-of-day evaluation to see if your time is being adequately devoted to your true priorities. If there is a gap between what you say and what you do, develop a schedule that puts you where you need to be to stay in alignment.

As you grow as a leader, you will need to continually remind yourself of your core values and who you really want to be. Don't try to be all things to all people. Focus instead on being your best self. When you do that and are intentional about anchoring your leadership in your core values, it will be easy to cultivate and maintain your credibility.

WHERE WILL YOU LEAD?

A lot of times, people think of leaders as the "out front" people, or the ones with the big, infectious personalities. But leaders are simply change agents, whether that results from being out front or behind the scenes. Not only do leaders effect change in circumstances, but they also effect change in people. I like to say that leaders are simply empowerment specialists. I believe that every person has the capacity to empower others and be a great leader.

EVERY PERSON HAS THE CAPACITY TO EMPOWER OTHERS AND BE A GREAT LEADER.

You may be reading this and saying, "I know there's more inside of me. I can see myself as a leader. I desire to create change in the world around me, but I just don't know how. I don't really know what I should be doing." If that's you, I believe that if you pay attention, you can quickly discover how you can be an effective change agent.

You may already know how your strengths and passions could be used to effect change. If so, great! Rise up and be a leader in that area. But if you are uncertain about how you could make a difference, take some time to consider the questions below. Your answers will help you discover where your leadership—or your service—is most needed:

- What stirs your passion?
- What do you desire to see changed?
- When you are driving around town, listening to the radio, or letting your mind drift, what catches your attention and stirs your emotions?
- What causes you to say to yourself something like, "Why isn't someone doing something about that?"

Well, that "someone" is *you*. If you've found something that makes you passionate—either angry or sad or especially enthusiastic—that is where your leadership is needed most.

In the next chapter, we'll go deeper into the leadership conversation. We've discussed some of the how-tos of developing the characteristics of an authentic, empowered leader. We'll look at why servant-leaders are perhaps the most powerful of all change agents.

WINNING ACTION: *LEARNING FROM LEADERS*

Think back to a time when someone's leadership dramatically affected your life—for good or for bad. Journal about that experience.

What did you learn from it?

How can you take those lessons and either replicate them or avoid them with others?

Meditate on the following poem entitled, "Anyway," and write your thoughts about it:

> *People are often unreasonable, illogical, and self-centered;*
> *Forgive them anyway.*
> *If you are kind, people may accuse you of selfish, ulterior*
> *motives;*
> *Be kind anyway.*
> *If you are successful, you will win some false friends and*
> *some true enemies;*
> *Succeed anyway.*
> *If you are honest and frank, people may cheat you;*
> *Be honest and frank anyway.*
> *What you spend years building, someone could destroy*
> *overnight;*
> *Build anyway.*
> *If you find serenity and happiness, they may be jealous;*

Be happy anyway.
The good you do today, people will often forget tomorrow;
   Do good anyway.
Give the world the best you have, and it may never be
   enough;
   Give the world the best you've got anyway.
You see, in the final analysis, it is between you and your God;
   It was never between you and them anyway.[89]

Chapter 11

SERVE TO WIN

"Develop the reputation of integrity, so no matter where you go, you will represent your family well or represent your company well. Your goal is success in the service of others, not at the expense of others. At the end of your road, you want to be able to say, "I fought a good fight, I finished the job, and I kept the faith."

-JIM ROHN, *LEADING AN INSPIRED LIFE*

When I was growing up, I thought a leader was a person who had a title or a position of authority. In my childish mind, I believed a leader was someone you saluted or bowed to. I thought leadership was all about directing and controlling others. Then I met the Benjamins and *everything* changed.

I've already told you that I grew up in poverty. One of life's difficulties for me was articulating the greatness I felt resided within me. I never felt isolated due to our circumstances, but knew intuitively we were different. All of the people in our community were homeowners—except us. All of the kids I knew lived with both of their parents—except us. All of the people around me had plenty, or at least enough. But not us. At one point we were in such a humble state that we not only ran out of food; we ran out of water. Poverty withheld the most basic essentials from our lives.

My mother was a single parent trying desperately to make ends meet. She did her best and taught us so many good things, but the reality is, my siblings and I were on a course to become statistics—warnings for others of what happens when life goes awry.

Then Mr. and Mrs. Benjamin came along.

The Benjamins served our community in tangible and intangible ways. They began by meeting my family's physical needs. Their generosity, even if it was just making sure we had water, was significant. But it was their example of servant-leadership that made an indelible impact on me. They were the catalyst that motivated our community to act for the good of all. They challenged us all to be better citizens by their own example of recognizing needs and reaching out to help those who had them.

The Benjamins' service to our family lifted the oppressive lid off of my social, spiritual, academic, and financial beliefs. Because of them, I no longer felt alone or disempowered—I understood my own inherent potential to lead through service...as a servant-leader. Empowered by hope, I was able to see greater possibilities for my future.

I'm sure this couple had no idea how powerful their example was to me or my siblings. They had no way of knowing that when they were serving our community—and in particular, my family—with their generosity, acts of kindness, and words of encouragement, that one small girl in the Trimm family, little Cindy, would one day honor their memory in front of thousands of people across the globe. However, the Benjamins didn't serve others to gain recognition; they served because they knew they could make a difference in our community—one family...one little girl...at a time.

As you've seen, *anyone* can be a leader and have influence in other people's lives. And when you focus your efforts on serving rather than on receiving, you can accomplish great feats on behalf of your family, workplace, and community. You can turn things around, not just for yourself, but for the entire world through your service, if even to just a few. That's what being a *servant*-leader is all about.

WHAT IS SERVANT-LEADERSHIP?

At first glance, the words *servant* and *leader* seem to contradict each other. Conventional wisdom suggests that servants wait on those in command and respond to their desires. Leaders, on the other hand, are those waited upon, who use their power and authority to make commands about what they desire. Truly great leaders, however, combine their power and authority with a purpose to serve. Servant-leaders pursue the good of those they serve above their own. Ken Keith, the CEO of the Greenleaf Center for Servant Leadership, explains it this way, "Servant leaders focus on identifying and meeting the needs of others rather than trying to acquire power, wealth, and fame for themselves."[90]

> TRULY GREAT LEADERS COMBINE THEIR POWER AND AUTHORITY WITH A PURPOSE TO SERVE.

Becoming a servant-leader does not depend on power or position, but it can be found wherever a person's influence is used to care for others. Servant-leadership isn't a step-by-step approach to leading. It isn't a tactic or a system. Like authenticity, transparency, impeccability, and many of the other concepts I've presented in *Unstoppable: Compete with Yourself and Win*, service is not simply a way of leading; it is a way of *being*. The characteristics of a servant-leader cannot (or at least *should not*) be turned on and off to suit the individual. They should be lived—day in and day out.

CHARACTERISTICS OF A SERVANT-LEADER

1. **Listening**—Servant-leaders listen to understand others' needs and desires.
2. **Empathy**—Servant-leaders strive to understand how other people think and feel.
3. **Healing**—Servant-leaders work with those they lead to create wholeness.
4. **Awareness**—Servant-leaders are perceptive of others' cir-

cumstances and needs. They are also self-aware, cognizant of how they come across to others.

5. **Persuasion**—Rather than use authority or power to push their agenda, servant-leaders work to build consensus.

6. **Conceptualization**—Servant-leaders aim to look at situations from varied perspectives. They dream and consider long-range possibilities without losing sight of their organization or community's immediate needs.

7. **Foresight**—Servant-leaders learn from the past and the present to plan for the future.

8. **Stewardship**—Servant-leaders are responsible for preparing their organization to make a contribution for the greater good.

9. **Commitment to the growth of people**—Servant-leaders are continually focused on helping their people develop personally and professionally.

10. **Community building**—Servant-leaders work to foster a sense of community and support among the members of the organization.

A BRIEF HISTORY OF SERVANT-LEADERSHIP

Robert Greenleaf, the "father of servant-leadership," wasn't the type of person you would expect to change the world. Laidback and unassuming, with a wry sense of humor, he listened more than he spoke. He spent his career in management research at AT&T and later as a respected university lecturer. In 1970, his short essay, "The Servant as Leader," introduced the world to the term "servant-leadership."

This simple idea transformed conventional thinking about leadership. Decades later, the servant model continues to inspire a new generation of leaders.

Greenleaf believed that leaders, at any level of an organization, have an obligation to nurture their followers and the communities they serve. In his view, servanthood is the driving motivation for leadership itself. "The servant-leader is servant first. It begins with the natural feeling that one wants to serve, to serve first," he explained. In Greenleaf's paradigm for servant leadership, the conscious choice to serve first takes priority over other power-driven or material desires. "The difference manifests itself in the care taken by the servant first to make sure that other people's highest priority needs are being served," he wrote in his bestselling book, *Servant Leadership: A Journey into the Nature of Legitimate Power and Greatness.*

WHY SERVE WHEN YOU CAN LEAD?

Servant-leadership is a long-term approach to life and work. It's a philosophy with the aim to create positive change throughout a group, community, or organization. It requires a commitment to:

- Lead by example, not just by words.
- Lead sacrificially by putting the needs of others before your own.
- Choose mercy over justice whenever possible.
- Build and promote others, rather than yourself.

Honestly, when you consider these requirements, servant-leadership looks like a lot of work! You may even ask, "Why bother being a servant-leader? Why not just be a leader and solve all the problems?"

Those aren't bad questions. After all, a leader could have a family's or a community's best interests at heart. With pure motives and the best intentions, he or she believes it is for the good of all to forcefully coerce others to achieve goals—that the ends will justify the means. That's certainly one way to operate. In fact, we've all seen that tactic taken repeatedly in politics, in nonprofit organizations, in corporations, and even in families. But there are a few major problems with this approach:

- People are not inspired to make a heart change even if their behavior is required to change. Most people resent changes that are *forced* upon them. That resentment may even cause followers to sabotage a leader's well-intended program.
- People become dependent when leaders don't allow them to participate in decision-making. To an authoritarian leader, that may sound ideal. The trouble comes when people abdicate responsibility for their actions, results, or well-being. Leadership then becomes a burden of responding to constant emergencies rather than helping people achieve their potential to problem-solve.
- Self-protection is the result of a bulldozer-type of leadership style, discouraging collaborative problem-solving. Rather than concerning themselves with the well-being or success of the community, followers focus more on their own need for survival.

Servant-leadership encourages people to grow, think, plan, and become engaged as part of the solution. And as was the case with the Benjamins and their impact on our community, servant-leadership is catalytic: It releases the community's potential by developing servants at every level. As Greenleaf explains, "All that is needed to rebuild community...is for enough servant-leaders to show the way, not by mass movements, but by each servant leader demonstrating his own unlimited liability for a quite specific community-related group."[91]

SERVANT-LEADERSHIP ENCOURAGES PEOPLE TO GROW, THINK, PLAN, AND BECOME ENGAGED AS PART OF THE SOLUTION.

Why serve when you can simply lead? Because service empowers you—and everyone you lead—to bring about more significant and lasting change than any amount of pressure or forced action ever could.

HOW CAN YOU BE AN EFFECTIVE SERVANT-LEADER?

"Everybody can be great because anybody can serve. You don't have to have a college degree to serve. You don't have to make your subject and your verb agree to serve.... You don't have to know the second theory of thermodynamics in physics to serve. You only need a heart full of grace. A soul generated by love."

-MARTIN LUTHER KING JR.

I hope by now you are convinced that true leadership is really servant-leadership. This practice in which I'm encouraging you to participate isn't simply about getting things done or earning a profit. While neither accolade-focused goals or financial goals are bad, they are inconsequential when compared with the goal of making the world a better place. I hope, too, you are convinced that servant-leadership, though not as expedient as demanding immediate action, can be far more effective in engaging everyone in creating positive, long-lasting results.

Perhaps you are in a position of authority now and need to make some shifts toward practicing a more service-oriented approach to leadership. Or maybe you want to use your strengths and unique gifts to serve others but aren't sure where to start. Regardless of where you are in your leadership journey, if you will increase your awareness of others and focus on coaching people rather than controlling their behavior, you can improve your effectiveness as a servant-leader.

INCREASE YOUR AWARENESS

One of the most important qualities for a servant-leader is awareness. You must be clued in to what is going on not only in your own life, but also in your environment. Awareness gives you insight into how you need to grow personally and professionally so you can effectively engage and empower others. Awareness also awakens you to the problems and needs of others. You can't serve people until you know what their needs are.

So, how can you become more aware?

1. **Ask thoughtful questions and listen for the answer.** It's common, especially for leaders, to ask a question and then jump into problem-solving mode without taking time to listen for the answer. Slow down and really listen.

2. **Practice being present.** If your attention is focused on the meeting you have next week or the deadline you have next month, it can be very difficult to be "in the moment." But that's where people live. Your family, friends, teammates, and followers need your full attention.

3. **People watch.** Have you ever sat in your workplace, your living room, or the food court in your local mall and just watched how others behave and interact? Being observant will allow you to spot needs that people may not verbally express.

COACH RATHER THAN CONTROL

Servant-leaders are keenly focused on *empowering* others to be their best. That means the objective isn't to force someone to buy in to *your* agenda, but rather to shepherd them toward their *own* best opportunities and outcomes. The goal is to coach people, rather than control them. Great coaches believe in their players and encourage, instruct, or exhort them to reach their peak performance level. The next time you're tempted to control someone's behavior, consider how you can come alongside him or her to gently provide direction. Asking questions that allow them to discover the right path will be far more effective than simply pointing the way.

Coaches engage the people they lead to learn how to help them thrive. Make time to discuss the following questions with the people you influence. If you have children, adapt the questions to suit their needs:

- What am I doing that helps you succeed?
- What am I not doing that you need in order to succeed?
- Where and how am I micromanaging you?
- When do you feel most encouraged and empowered?

Measure Success As a Servant-Leader

While some analysts measure a leader's success by the growth of their stock or the number of their followers on Twitter, Greenleaf argued for a different standard. The questions he asked ensured that people's lives (not just their immediate circumstances) were improved. Greenleaf asked:

- "Do those served grow as persons?"
- "Do they, while being served, become healthier, wiser, freer, more autonomous, more likely themselves to become servants?'
- "What is the effect on the least privileged in society? Will they benefit, or at least not be further deprived?"

FROM THE BOARDROOM TO THE LIVING ROOM

Few people make it out of school without being bullied. Looking back, you may remember kids humiliating an unpopular student or times when you were afraid to run into a bully after school. "No matter what high school you go to, what age you are, what social group you're in, you've been bullied and you are a bully," explains one high school student. "Once you start realizing that you can have higher social power by putting other people down . . . that's, like, how people are moving up and that's how they're gaining respect."

As this student observed, bullying reflects a basic desire for status and power, and while schools try various strategies to eliminate the

MORE THAN EVER, WE NEED YOUNG PEOPLE WHO WILL INFLUENCE THEIR PEERS THROUGH SERVANT-LEADERSHIP.

problem, the best deterrent to schoolyard bullying is students who bring courage and kindness to the situation. More than ever, we need young people who will influence their peers through servant-leadership.

It's never too early for a child to learn how to serve, claims Pat Williams, senior vice president of the NBA's Orlando Magic. As the father of nineteen children, fourteen of whom are adopted, Williams has seen the power of peer leadership firsthand. "When young people see leadership as a form of servanthood rather than a way of boosting their power, status, and egos, their entire view of life and their place in life will be transformed,"[92] he says. Training your children to become servant-leaders changes the course of their own lives and the lives of their peers.

In his book, *Coaching Your Kids to Be Leaders: The Keys to Unlocking Their Potential*, Williams offers seven principles parents can use to instill servant leadership in their children. In addition to setting an example of servant-leadership at home, parents who train their children to serve prepare them for a lifetime of influence.

SEVEN PRINCIPLES FOR RAISING SERVANT-LEADERS

1. **Help children give up the need to control.** Teach kids to deal with performance pressures, so they can take on future responsibilities without freezing up or trying to control the situation. Help them see that it's okay to fail.

2. **Train them to see servanthood as an end, not a means to an end.** Don't let them use service to manipulate people to get their way. Instead, teach them to give without expecting anything in return. As Williams explains, "Servanthood is not a technique, it's a way of life."

3. **Ask young leaders to examine their motives.** Why do they want to lead? If you see that a young person is hungry for power or concerned with their popularity, step in and share your observations. Williams's friend, football coach John Mackovic, explains it this way:

> Young people should know that leadership is difficult—pain and sacrifice come with it, and it should only be approached with the right motives. Those young leaders who crave the attention and admiration that often come with leadership should be handled with caution. They need to be reminded of the need for humility. They need to learn that the real reward for leadership is not an inflated ego, but the satisfaction of the accomplishment of the team.

4. **Model a lifestyle of love and caring.** Expose your kids to real-world needs and create opportunities for them to respond. One of the best ways for them to learn is to serve alongside you.

5. **Teach them to be an obedient follower.** "Learn to obey before you command," advised the Greek philosopher Solon. Look for opportunities to expose young people to servant-leaders, and don't put them in positions of leadership before they have learned to follow.

6. **Make humility the goal.** This principle goes hand in hand with learning to follow. Express pride in young people for who they are, rather than for what they achieve. Let them know you are their biggest fan as you encourage service over self.

7. **Encourage your children to "get their shoulders dirty."** Remind young people of the people who have supported them as they've grown and challenge them to do the same for others. As Williams explains, "Servant leaders are always

lifting people up and letting them stand tall on their shoulders. Servant leaders don't care who gets the glory and recognition; they just want to lift people up."[93]

Imagine the impact a new generation of servant-leaders could have on our world! It's never too early to teach children to serve, so start now.

WHAT'S IN IT FOR YOU?

Throughout our discussion of servant-leadership, you've been challenged to consider others' needs before your own. However, it is human nature to wonder, "What's in it for me?"

As you've seen, leadership is not for the faint of heart—it requires you to surrender your own ego and ambition as you consider the needs of others. At the same time, the process of becoming a servant-leader will develop a confidence and a resiliency that cannot be developed any other way. Robert Greenleaf reflected on the change that happens in leaders' lives as they learn to serve:

To lead is to go out ahead and show the way when the way may be unclear, difficult, or dangerous—it is not just walking at the head of the parade—and that one who leads effectively is likely to be stronger, more self-assured, and more resourceful than most because leading so often involves venturing and risking.[94] What a powerful sentiment. Because leading so often involves venturing and risking, it will make

> CELEBRATE THE CHANGES YOU SEE AS YOUR INFLUENCE AND DEPTH OF CHARACTER GROW.

you stronger, more self-assured, and more resourceful than most! As you begin this journey toward servant-leadership, remember that growth is a process; challenge yourself to a higher standard, but give yourself the grace and time you need to mature. Along the way, celebrate the changes you see as your influence and depth of character grow.

WINNING ACTION: *WHOM DO YOU SERVE?*

Remember, servant-leadership does not depend on a title or position but on a heart willing to respond to a need. When your motivation is first to serve, then to lead—or to lead through service—you will continually increase your capacity to impact your community, company, or family for the greatest good.

Specifically identify...

- The circle of influence where you will be intentional about serving others
- The type of service you will offer
- The actions or responsibility you will take
- The outcome of your service-oriented actions
- The way your service will help others be healthier, stronger, and more independent

Chapter 12

LEAVE A WINNING LEGACY

"What we do for ourselves dies with us.
What we do for others and the world remains and is immortal."

-ALBERT PIKE

Most people don't like to think about death. We'd much rather spend our time focusing on life: how to prolong it, enrich it, and enjoy it. But death? That can wait.

Perhaps it's because we focus so much on life that death always comes as a surprise. Even when we've looked through the peephole and seen death standing outside the door wearing the garb of terminal disease or simply old age, it always seems shocking when that door is opened—and then closed one final time. Suddenly there are no more chances to say:

"I love you."

"I'm proud of you."

"You are precious to me."

The lucky among us beat the average and live well into their eighties and nineties. But it is the best among us who determine early on to make every day count—whether the days are few or many. Those people—the ones who "suck the marrow out of life,"[95] who love fully and authentically, who passionately practice uplifting others—are the ones who live well beyond their years because of the legacy they leave.

"Nobody is truly gone until all those who are touched or influenced by that person are gone," commented Appleseed Recording founder Jim Musselman, when folk singer and activist Pete Seeger passed away at the age of ninety-four in early 2014. That truth allows each of us the possibility to live in the hearts and minds of those we touch with our unique brand of service, leadership, and even love. In this final chapter of *Unstoppable: Compete with Yourself and Win*, we'll look at how you can invest your time, energy, and passion so that when your life draws to a close, your legacy will live on.

WHAT IS A LEGACY?

Often, the word *legacy* is associated with high-profile celebrities, activists, and politicians. In recent years, the media have focused our attention on the lives and deaths of people such as Ruth Bader Ginsburg, Kobe Bryant, Prince Philip, Chadwick Boseman, and Larry King—and not that long ago, Steve Jobs, Nelson Mandela, Princess Diana, and Margaret Thatcher. Each of these individuals left an impressive mark on the world.

YOUR LEGACY IS ABOUT STARTING A RIPPLE EFFECT THAT CONTINUALLY CREATES CHANGE-MAKERS.

Their cultural influence, inspiration, message, and example made an impact on millions of people's lives. But for all these individuals' noteworthy accomplishments, the reality is that who they were mattered far more than what they did or how much they accumulated. That's why legacy isn't relegated to the rich and famous. Your life—who you are, the relationships you build, and how you serve others with generosity and kindness—though perhaps unnoticed by the media, is what makes the most far-reaching and tremendous impact.

You see, legacy isn't about fame or fortune. (So, if you were fearful you'd have to make stage appearances or talk to the press to make a difference, you can relax!) It is about being your best now, so you can empower others, so they can empower others, so they can empower others—your legacy is about starting a ripple effect that continually creates change-makers. It's leaving in your wake an unstoppable force for good.

Stephen R. Covey explained that the desire to leave a legacy is innate. "There are certain things that are fundamental to human fulfillment," Covey wrote in *First Things First*.

> The essence of these needs is captured in the phrase 'to live, to love, to learn, to leave a legacy.' The need to live is our physical need for such things as food, clothing, shelter, economic wellbeing, and health. The need to love is our social need to relate to other people, to belong, to love, and to be loved. The need to learn is our mental need to develop and to grow. And the need to leave a legacy is our spiritual need to have a sense of meaning, purpose, personal congruence, and contribution.[96]

Sometimes people misunderstand legacy and think it's a prideful desire to leave a mark on society. But when you define legacy as I do—*the desire to use your unique gifts to fulfill your purpose for the betterment of others*—there's nothing selfish about it. In fact, it can be the greatest and most humble gift you can offer.

WHAT DOES IT TAKE TO LEAVE A LEGACY?

"Live today the way you want to be remembered tomorrow."

-DILLON BURROUGHS

Dobri Dobrev, at the age of ninety-nine, continued to make his way each day from his village into the city of Sophia, Bulgaria. There, in his traditional handmade folk attire and worn leather shoes, he begged for money.

Grandpa Dobri, as he was affectionately called by locals, was well-known in the community. People there respected his gentle voice, and were perhaps a bit amused by his bushy white beard and habit of kissing the hands of those who shared their money. He was recognized, certainly, because he spent so much time holding out his money box on the city's streets. But he was *known* because he gave away all the money he collected.

Since 2000, Dobrev collected, coin by coin, enough to give away more than $50,000. The money has helped to rebuild churches and monasteries, to pay utility bills for orphanages, and to assist a myriad of others in need. When church officials at the St. Alexander Nevsky Cathedral in Sofia checked the donation ledger, they were shocked to learn that the largest contributor was a "poor, old man."

Dobrev, who survived on his government pension (about $100/month) and gifts of food from strangers, made quite an impression in Bulgaria where he's been dubbed a saint. His humble spirit, his eagerness to share his faith, and his generosity both surprised and challenged members of his community to do and *be* more themselves. He was not famous, nor did he want to be, but his legacy will be remembered long after his death.[97] Dobrev understood what so many people miss. The material goods passed on to the next generation matter little compared to the example you set for them while you're alive. Grandpa Dobrev died at the age of 103.

Following the funeral services for the twelve men and women who were killed in the Washington Navy Yard shooting in September 2013, Arianna Huffington wrote a poignant post titled "Are You Living Your Eulogy or Your Résumé?" In it, she noted that the eulogies, the documentation of the victims' lives, didn't highlight their work accomplishments or their dedication to the office. Rather, the words spoken to honor these individuals shared who they were as husbands and wives, fathers, mothers, sons, daughters, and friends.

"No matter how much a person spends his or her life burning the candle at both ends, chasing a toxic definition of success and generally missing out on life, the eulogy is always about the other stuff: What they gave, how they connected, how much they meant to the lives of the real people around them, small kindnesses, life-long passions, and what made them laugh,"[98] Huffington wrote. So, the question is: *Why do we spend so much time on what our eulogy is* not *going to be?*

Why, indeed. For most of my life, I thought if I *did* more, and if I *got* more, it would really make a difference in my status, and my feeling of significance. I thought what I learned and experienced would give me the ultimate understanding of who I am as an individual. And so I spent the first part of my life not having a clear sense of what was genuine for me—true to my own deepest desires, values, and identity. I let other people's expectations determine my goals. What looked like success or "achievement" or even "enough" to others was not satisfying to me—because what defined those things for me didn't match other people's definitions. I wanted more than a position or title, I wanted more than a high-ranking political office, I wanted to know I was changing lives. I wanted to leave a wake of empowered individuals, communities, even regions, with the insights I'd known had changed my life. Those insights dictated that I *be* the change I wanted to see. I learned that what made the most impact was more about who I was and the people I connected with than any singular accomplishment. My work and gift to the world is being the best me I can be—

> SUCCESS ISN'T ABOUT WHAT WE DO; IT'S ABOUT WHO WE ARE AND WHO WE INFLUENCE.

competing with no one but myself and demonstrating the power of living and leading authentically in the process—because the more authentic I am in every encounter, whether speaking, coaching, advising, or simply connecting with the individuals I meet around the world—the more empowerment that results on all levels.

Success isn't about what we *do*; it's about who we *are* and who we influence. To do more, I simply have to be more and more true to who I am and why I'm here—whatever shape and form that takes. That's what it means to *compete with yourself and win!* And that's what is required to leave a legacy that empowers others to win.

HOW WILL YOU SHAPE YOUR LEGACY?

If creating a legacy is based on being rather than on doing, how can you intentionally shape your legacy? You do it by:

- Knowing who you are.
- Living with integrity.
- Being authentic and transparent.
- Positively influencing people by adding value to their lives.
- Leading others and yourself with excellence.
- Serving others unselfishly.
- Fulfilling your purpose by maximizing your unique gifts, strengths, and abilities.

Most importantly, remember that your legacy and your life *now* are best crafted when you commit to living out each of those concepts every day, with every person you encounter. I challenge you to be intentional in your life and in defining your legacy. Identify your purpose and then devote your life to achieving it. The world will be better for it.

IDENTIFY YOUR PURPOSE

"The purpose of life is not to be happy. It is to be useful, to be honorable, to be compassionate, to have it make some difference that you have lived and lived well."
-RALPH WALDO EMERSON

One of our greatest missions is to make a difference in this world. How we do that varies from person to person based on our skills, talents, and abilities. Not all of us paint or sing or speak publicly or write books or manage corporations or raise children. We all have different methods of going about fulfilling our mission to make a difference.

Each one of us has a why—the reason that drives our thoughts and actions. That "why" is your mission—that's your purpose. My desire is to leave a legacy of hope, meaning, and dignity for the next generation. I'm building that legacy now through my mission of empowering people to discover purpose and maximize potential.

You'll notice that my mission isn't about money or notoriety. It is about others, because I believe that service to others is the only real way to create a life of significance—one whose impact endures beyond our selves.

To intentionally design your legacy, you must first identify your life's mission—your purpose, your reason for being. Nothing exists without purpose. Some believe purpose is determined by a higher power. I believe that higher power is God. Yet, although God determines purpose, it must be discovered by you.

I've always been inspired by a story Winston Churchill tells of his youth. He describes how when he was sixteen, he and a friend were discussing their futures after chapel one Sunday evening. Churchill professed to his friend that he had a clear vision of his purpose. As recorded in several biographies, he stated, "This country will be subjected somehow to a tremendous invasion, by what means I do not know, but I tell you I shall be in command of the defenses of London, and I shall save London and England from disaster...In the high position I shall occupy, it will fall to me to save the Capital and save the Empire."[99] He not only sensed the gravitas of his purpose, but more extraordinarily, he could articulate it with precision.

How about you? Do you know why you are here? Do you know your reason for being? So many people struggle with knowing their purpose. If you're among those who are still searching, here are a few questions that might help you nail it down:

1. What are you passionate about?
2. What is the one thing that you do best?
3. If you could only do one thing, what would that be?
4. What makes you feel truly fulfilled?

Your purpose and your passion are inextricably connected. When you can identify what thrills you, what gets you up in the morning or keeps you up late at night, what you would do even if

YOUR PURPOSE AND YOUR PASSION ARE INEXTRICABLY CONNECTED.

you never earned a dime for it—then you've found your purpose and passion.

Take a few moments now to think about your purpose. Answer the questions above. Using what you discover about yourself, draft your mission statement.

TAKE A STAND

Although having a clear sense of purpose is empowering, it also poses challenges. It takes courage to say "no" to opportunities that are not "on purpose"—or to distinguish which will put you on the main road to fulfilling your purpose, and which only run parallel. And then there are the risks, obstacles, opinions of other people, and uncertainties that will threaten to knock you off course. To thrive, to fulfill your mission, to leave a legacy that will empower others, you must choose to take a stand. You will need the critical three Cs: courage, commitment, and confidence.

If you don't feel very courageous, or if you have trouble seeing projects through to the end, or if you just aren't sure you have what is required to complete your mission, take heart! Like every other character trait we've identified in *Unstoppable: Compete with Yourself and Win*, courage, commitment, and confidence can be developed with practice. Let's take a look at each of the three Cs and how you can strengthen their presence in your life.

COURAGE

Courage is not the absence of fear; it is the willingness to feel the fear and act in spite of it. With it, you can find the strength to create stronger relationships and to embark on new, and sometimes scary, endeavors. Without it, life can seem pretty lonely and uninteresting.

Theologian Mary Daly is quoted for her wisdom on how to push beyond your fears: "Courage is…a habitus, a habit, a virtue: You get it by courageous acts. It's like you learn to swim by swimming. You learn courage by *couraging*."[100]

Courage requires practice. Maybe that's why Eleanor Roosevelt advised, "Do one thing every day that scares you." Every time you take a stand for your purpose and your beliefs, you become a bit more emboldened. And like every other positive virtue you display, your courage rubs off on other people. In *The Gifts of Imperfection*, Brené Brown describes the empowering effect our courage has on others: "Every time we choose courage, we make everyone around us a little better and the world a little braver. And our world could stand to be a little kinder and braver."[101]

Many of the most important contributions ever made were made by people who had the courage to act. It doesn't matter whether the world perceives your work as small or great. What matters is that you have the courage to act. It's okay to feel the fear. Acknowledge it. Then, be courageous and push right through it.

COMMITMENT

Everything rises and falls on your commitment—your dedication to seeing your mission completed.

Commitment is a word that's too often tossed around without much thought. For example, a person may say they're in a "committed" relationship, but they bail when times get tough and/ or when a more interesting proposal comes along. We hear (and say) the term *overcommitted* in respect to busy schedules as an excuse to bow out of "commitments."

So, how do we prevent the word *commitment* from being lip service? One way is to define the terms and the desired outcome. In terms of your life's purpose and the legacy you will leave, consider the following questions:

- To what exactly are you committing?
- To what or whom are you dedicating your life?
- What are the desired results for you?
- What are the desired results for others?

Know exactly what you're getting into before you commit. This is your purpose and your legacy, so you have the power and the freedom to define the terms. However, once you make the commitment, determine to live with integrity. Keep your promise to fulfill your purpose.

CONFIDENCE

Sometimes confidence is perceived as arrogance. But remember, your legacy, and thus your purpose, is not about a selfish or prideful existence. If your true and pure aim is to serve others, then you must realize there is nothing helpful about living small so people feel better about themselves. In fact, you are doing the people around you a great disservice if you offer up anything less than your very best self.

You may be familiar with this powerful quote from Marianne Williamson's bestselling book *A Return to Love*. Williamson so expertly captures the real crux of confidence; it isn't about you, it's about the difference you can make with your light.

Our deepest fear is not that we are inadequate. Our deepest fear is that we are powerful beyond measure. It is our light, not our darkness that most frightens us. We ask ourselves, *"Who am I to be brilliant, gorgeous, talented, and fabulous?"* Actually, who are you not to be? You are a child of God. Your playing small does not serve the world. There is nothing enlightened about shrinking so that other people will not feel insecure around you. We are all meant to shine, as children do. We were born to make manifest the glory of God that is within us. It is not just in some of us; it is in everyone and as we let our own light shine, we unconsciously give others permission to do the same. As we are liberated from our own fear, our presence automatically liberates others.[102]

I want to challenge you to do something great. Leave a legacy by refusing to blend in. Stand out, stand up!

Leave your footprint, your voiceprint, and your thumbprint behind so that the next generation knows that you did something beyond your comfort zone. *You* have the power to change not only yourself, but also the world around you.

> YOU HAVE THE POWER TO CHANGE NOT ONLY YOURSELF, BUT ALSO THE WORLD AROUND YOU.

 WINNING ACTION: *WRITE YOUR EULOGY*

As we close out this last chapter in your journey to compete with yourself and win, I want to challenge you to think about your legacy. What will people remember about you when you're gone? What about your life will be unstoppable even when you're no longer living it?

As you complete this exercise, remember that eulogies are not résumés. This is not about the companies you built, or the titles you wore—or how much money you leave behind. Nor is it about your inventions or innovations. People will care far less about where you worked and what you accomplished than about the kind of person you were and how you made them feel.

- What do you want others to say about your life?
- Whose lives did you improve and how?
- How did you serve or benefit others?
- Where did you make a difference?
- Who will live stronger, happier, and more fully because they knew you?

Conclusion

LIVING FROM THE INSIDE OUT

At the 2014 Winter Olympics in Sochi, Lolo Jones, a track and field athlete, tried something new, and lost. Or did she?

The thirty-year-old hurdler earned her spot as a brakeman on the U.S. Olympic bobsled team, the team she helped to win a gold in the 2013 World Championships. She joined the team after two back-to-back Olympic losses. (She placed fourth at the 2012 Summer Olympics in London and seventh in Beijing in 2008 after tripping on a hurdle.)

As she looked toward the 2014 Olympics, Jones commented that her losses fueled her decision to try for the winter games. "I've wondered how my life would have been different if I hadn't hit that hurdle in Beijing, or if I got that medal in London. But you know what? I'm pleased with the fact that, because it's so difficult, because I have so many really close failures to a medal, that if it does happen it's going to be one of the most amazing things. Because people know this struggle. People have lived this struggle with me."[103]

To get to the London Olympics, Jones says she fought through surgery and two hamstring tears. So, on the one hand, even though she didn't go home with a medal, she knew she had nothing to be ashamed of. "I wasn't even supposed to make that team, but I wish I had a medal! I didn't want to give up."[104]

She didn't want her dedication and training to be for nothing. So she temporarily turned her attention to a totally different sport: bobsledding.

Realistically, medaling as a bobsledder was a long shot for Jones. Still, she trained hard, supported her teammates, and packed on the pounds to meet her goal weight for the games. And when she and her driver took eleventh in the finals, she didn't seem devastated. In fact, she didn't miss a beat. The finish line photos show her brilliant smile as she hugged her teammates who won the silver and bronze medals. Instead of mourning her defeat, she celebrated her team's victories.

She didn't take home an Olympic medal, but the friendships, and the physical and mental strength she gained from the games, seemed to have renewed her energy. Only a few days after the 2014 winter games ended, she posted a Facebook comment that she was back to running, looking forward to the next track and field season.

Certainly, this young woman competes for herself, but she also knows that every time she picks herself up, she inspires others to keep trying for their own goals. "I hope people can see and be inspired by my journey of perseverance and not giving up," she says. "That's every Olympic athlete's dream—to win a medal, but also to be an inspiration for those watching back home."[105]

When we began this life-transformation journey together, I told you I believe it's possible for you to experience a bigger, bolder, and more meaningful life. My hope is that you caught a glimpse of that possibility as you discovered (or perhaps rediscovered) your true identity and what your life's purpose is. But I also hope you see that although you compete with yourself to win, your competition isn't only about you. The example you set by getting up when you fall, by humbling yourself when you fail, and by winning when you stay true to your authentic self all inspire others to go for their dreams.

One life can change the world.

Let your life be the one.

THE WINNING STREAK

How to win at everything in life!

The ability to win is in all of us.

Unfortunately, winning is not an everyday phenomenon because so many people stay stuck at the starting line or stop right on the brink of a win. Convinced they don't have the skill, or have run out of steam, they don't reach deeper into their potential to find that second wind. Mahatma Gandhi said, "Strength doesn't come from physical capacity. It comes from an indomitable will."[106] And Arnold Schwarzenegger said, "Strength doesn't come from winning. Your struggles develop your strengths. When you go through hardships and decide not to surrender, that is strength."[107]

Most of us are stronger and more talented than we give ourselves credit for. Yes, we all have that inner critic telling us to give up—but we don't have to listen. Your feelings don't know how powerful and strong you truly are. Tony Dungy said, "Winners win...[those] who won all the way through high school and college, the best player at every level, they have a way of making things happen and winning games."[108] Your soul knows the terrain of your destiny—the terrain of being a winner!

Every day you are given the opportunity to let go of your fears, shatter self-imposed limitations, dig deeper, push harder, and shift from a primal state to a powerful state so you can recognize opportunities, let go of insecurities, and stop listening to what others say about what you can accomplish. Every day you can decide to own every moment of your life—to leave nothing to chance. When you choose to live intentionally, before long you will have owned the hour, the day, the month, the year, and the decade. And that's how you win at life. That's how you become *unstoppable*!

It doesn't happen all at once; it happens incrementally—step by step, little by little, one foot in front of the other; saying "no" to the wrong things so you can say "yes" to the right ones. When it comes to winning, there are no off-seasons, no time clocks to stop the action, no referees telling you that you fouled or struck out. There are, however, endless challenges, disappointments, mistakes, roadblocks, barriers, and issues that force most people out of their own race. But if you stick with it, persist until you succeed, survive the battlefield in your mind to overcome self-sabotage and the seduction to give up or give in to your emotions, you *will* win!

Winning is the difference between dreaming about what could be and actually living the life of your dreams. Winning is a motivating force that drives you forward. Winning causes the steel bars of failure to independently shut behind you. They are real for all of us who have experienced the bitter reality of failing. For those who have convinced themselves that their past mistakes are a preview of their future, those bars become their prison. But for winners, those bars are a sign that a particular season has come to an end. They understand that nothing new begins until something old ends. Serena Williams, one of the most decorated female tennis players in the history of the sport, said, "If winning is God's reward, then losing is how He teaches us."[109] Michael Jordan said, "I've missed more than nine thousand shots in my career. I've lost almost three hundred games.

Twenty-six times I've been trusted to take the game-winning shot and missed. I've failed over and over and over again in my life. And that is why I succeed."[110]

From this day on, you must never go back to losing or failing—but instead, press forward, leveraging every loss and failure to your winning advantage. If you take 100 percent responsibility for making the most out of every opportunity—the good, the bad, and the ugly—you will win at living the life of your dreams.

DON'T BE DECEIVED

Failure never lies, but it always hides the truth. It tells you that everything you want is so close—just beyond your comfort zone—and then it laughs as it slams the doors of opportunity in your face. It tells you all your goals and dreams are impossible because you don't have the key to unlock the door, and then it taunts you if you try to open it, never informing you that when one door closes, another opens. Don't become so focused on the closed doors that you don't see the ones standing open. Don't go through life suffering from possibility blindness!

Unlike loudmouthed Failure, Winning speaks just above a whisper, causing you to lean in so you can tune out Failure's taunts and jeers. Failure is always rational and risk-averse, unforgiving if you mess up, taking every opportunity to remind you that you are not good enough, prepared enough, educated enough, pretty enough, strong enough…always reminding you that you will never be enough. It shows you your weakness and hangs your flaws out like dirty laundry. It reminds you every day that if anyone finds out who you really are, they will never want to do business with you, be your friend, hire you, or marry you. So, you live as a stranger to yourself. You wake up every morning like millions do and put on your mask and title, then go off to work and blend in with everyone else. Failure convinces you to quit trying because this is as good as it gets.

Winning, on the other hand, is a revealer of truth. It reveals the fact that you have it in you to win at life—to live better and do better; that greatness is in you. That you can go for your dreams—and that dreams do come true, because all things are possible for those who believe. Believe in yourself and in your dreams!

THE WINNER IN YOU

The winner in you is a cheerleader that cheers you along. She encourages you to take one more step to an uncertain destination that might not even be there when you get there, because when you get there, it will be vastly different and even better than you imagined—a whole new world. Winning is pure craziness. It tells you to jump and grow wings on the way down. It doesn't sleep, but it visits you in your dreams.

Emmitt Smith said, "For me, winning isn't something that happens suddenly on the field when the whistle blows and the crowds roar. Winning is something that builds physically and mentally every day that you train and every night that you dream."[111] Winning is like that beautiful dream you can't remember when you wake up, but you still feel the sensation of its caress. Winning is the infinite game. Dynamic in nature, it morphs into each individual's personal goals, visions, and dreams. You can't pin it down, and words may fail to describe it. But when you win, you know it. You feel it.

Winning doesn't care if you understand why you do the things you do, and even though it knows the answers to your questions, it doesn't always share those answers with you. Like a jealous lover, it refuses to share time, space, or its secrets for how and why you do what you do with others in your life, especially those who waste their time dreaming and never wake up to actually *live* the life of their dreams. Winning is not fond of procrastinators, but loves those who have a driving obsession and a relentless passion for completing a goal. Winning looks irrational and risky to others around you. But to you, winning makes sense.

Winning shows you the best of who you are, the strength in you, and the potential you have to be the next best version of yourself.

Winning keeps its hands behind its back, so it doesn't accidentally embrace someone who is lackadaisical, half-hearted, and unenthusiastic about their lives. Unlike Failure, who with open arms shows you the shortcuts for doing everything, Winning escorts you along the narrow path universally known as the long way home—filled with valley experiences. Winning watches over you, but never carries you. And when you, through sheer grit and will, manage to reach the mountain peak of success, Winning will be there to greet you with open arms and place upon you the winner's wreath, just before it pushes you off the edge because it knows that every win is fleeting. Once you win, the next moment presents another opportunity for yet another win. Mia Hamm said, "There are always new, grander challenges to confront, and a true winner will embrace each one."[112] Babe Ruth said, "Yesterday's homeruns don't win today's games."[113] And Vince Lombardi said, "Winning is not a sometime thing; it's an all-time thing. You don't win once in a while, you don't do things right once...you do them right all the time. Winning is a habit. Unfortunately, so is losing."[114]

Everything you want out of life can be attained, but you must get out of your comfort zone. You must wake up to your potential and put a lid on every self-imposed limitation.

If you can feel your fears, but do it anyway, tolerate the jarring emotional pain that comes with rejection, stomach letdowns, and betrayal; if you can motivate yourself in the midst of doubt and become your own best friend, coach, advocate, and chief inspirational officer in the midst of loneliness, disappointment, and frustration, then *unstoppable* will be what defines you and your personal brand. It will become the salient feature of your personality and the hallmark of your legacy.

Make *Unstoppable* your companion—and *Winning* your most intimate friend.

OWN IT TO WIN IT

Winning tells you to own your story—but more importantly, to be the hero of that story. Brené Brown said, "Owning your story can be hard, but not nearly as difficult as spending your life running from it."[115] You have been cast as the lead. Don't settle for playing a supporting role—or worse, that of a stand-in. Take center stage and step into the light of the world premiere of your life.

Winning demands that you live authentically, ridding yourself of false identities, personas, masks, and alter egos. It introduces you to the person you've been pretending to be, and then it shows you who you have the potential to be. Winning is like a devoted and affectionate lover who caresses your creative genius, strokes your talents, and massages your innovative abilities, who whispers in the ears of your potential, "Come alive, come alive." It robes its nakedness in the morning with passion, focus, and intention. Winning is unapologetic when it tells you, "You are a one-of-a-kind gift to humanity. You are enough. You can't be replaced. You can do this! Your life is important in the big scheme of things!"

Winning is filled with empathy, but the sense of urgency causes its compassionate glance to appear as a snarl easily interpreted as indifference or hostility—but it's not. The winner in you wants you to win so badly that it does not mind being misunderstood. One minute it will show you an opportunity; the next it will reveal a lesson, a weak point, or a step you missed behind you. It connects the dots between strategy and tactic. All Winning cares about is that you get to that mountaintop of success. Winning doesn't care if you run, walk, crawl, or drag yourself along its path. It doesn't care about how you feel at any given moment because it doesn't judge your greatness based on a temporary meltdown.

Winning never takes the struggle out of your stride because it knows that every time you push past the point of giving up, you build the muscle of character in the process. Winning holds you in such high esteem that it has already awarded you a place among the great. Your bloodied knees, sweat-laced brows, and calloused hands are integral parts of a badge called greatness, a badge all the greats have earned. They are those who have gone before you. They are those who have traveled the same paths you have. They are those who have scaled the same mountain peak of success you've yet to climb. From the corridors of history, they are the unseen company of witnesses who are cheering you on across the finish line.

Winning expresses itself as deep-down delight that emerges as tears of joy, disbelief, and gratitude. Winning floods your soul with the force of Niagara Falls. It is an overwhelming, awesome feeling of pure happiness and fullness—the feeling that makes you cover your face to keep from imploding with emotion. It's a feeling that makes your knees buckle. It makes you grin so big you feel your face will break—and your heart fill with such gratitude that it might explode. Your lungs refuse to exhale, wanting to savor the sweet fragrance and taste of success as long as humanly possible. Winning makes you speechless and breathless; it makes you want to jump, scream, and run to give your friends a high five and your loved ones a hug, because of the euphoric sense of blessedness that comes from accomplishment.

However elusive it may be, Winning is the mentor you've always wanted and the coach you've always needed. Winning is not just what you do but who you become in the process. And when you do score a win, you will connect once again with the feeling that accompanied your first win, and perhaps utter the words I often say to myself, *"This is how it feels to be unstoppable!"* And like me, you will have at last acquired the indomitable courage to perpetuate your own unique winning streak.

You inherently know what is best for you and how to win. And you can recapture that feeling throughout your entire life over and over again—with big wins and little wins.

You deserve to win. You were born to win! You are unstoppable! I therefore implore you to *compete with your best self and win!* Only when you are able to compete with your best self will you truly win… and only then will you become truly unstoppable!

ENDNOTES

1 Brené Brown, *I Thought It Was Just Me (But It Isn't): Making the Journey from "What Will People Think?" to "I Am Enough"* (United States: Gotham Books, 2008), viii.

2 Judith Orloff, "How to Stop Comparing Yourself to Others," http://www.huffingtonpost.com/judith-orloff-md/stop-comparing_b_1447174.html.

3 Exodus 20:1 HCSB.

4 Viktor Emil Frankl, *Man's Search for Meaning* (United Kingdom: Beacon Press, 1992), 113.

5 Viktor Emil Frankl, *Man's Search for Meaning* (United Kingdom: Pocket Books, 1985), 68.

6 James Allen, *As a Man Thinketh* (Camarillo, CA: DeVorss, 1948), 18–19.

7 Marci Shimoff, *Happy for No Reason: 7 Steps to Being Happy from the Inside Out* (United States: Atria Books, 2009), 83.

8 Romans 12:2 HCSB

9 Hara Estroff Marano, "Depression Doing the Thinking," *Psychology Today*, July 1, 2001, http://www.psychologytoday.com/articles/200308/depression-doing-the-thinking.

10 "Author Brené Brown Discusses Embracing Our Ordinariness," http://www.huffingtonpost.com/martha-rosenberg/embracing-our-ordinariness_b_802808.html.

11 https://www.inspirationalstories.com/emperors-seed-the/, retrieved May 26, 2021.

12 Oscar Wilde, gifted Irish poet, cited in Steve Farrar, *Finishing Strong* (United Kingdom: Crown Publishing, 2011), 153.

13 "Abraham Lincoln Online," http://www.abrahamlincolnonline.org/lincoln/speeches/house.htm.

14 *Online Etymology Dictionary*, http://www.etymonline.com/index.php?term=authentic.

15 *Merriam-Webster*, http://www.merriam-webster.com/dictionary/authenticity.

16 https://www.explorepsychology.com/barnum-effect, accessed May 22, 2021.

17 Darren Hardy, *The Compound Effect: Jumpstart Your Income, Your Life, Your Success* (United States: Hachette Books, 2020), 65.

18 Arianna Huffington, *Thrive: The Third Metric to Redefining Success and Creating a Life of Well-Being, Wisdom, and Wonder* (United States: Harmony/Rodale, 2014), 1.

19 Richard Barrett, *The Values Driven Organization* (United Kingdom: Routledge, 2014), iv.

20 Huffington, *Thrive*, 15.

21 Jack Canfield and Janet Switzer, *The Success Principles* (United States: HarperCollins, 2009), 5.

22 Lisa Wimberger, *New Beliefs, New Brain: Free Yourself from Stress and Fear* (United States: Divine Arts, 2012).

23 "Mayo Clinic: Stress Management," http://www.mayoclinic.org/healthy-living/stress-management/in-depth/stress/art-20046037.

24 Daniel J. Siegel, *Mindsight: The New Science of Personal Transformation* (United States: Bantam Books, 2010), xii.

25 Siegal, *Mindsight*, xii.

26 Randy Pausch, *The Last Lecture: Lessons in Living* (United Kingdom: Two Roads, 2010).

27 Harry Markopolos, *No One Would Listen: A True Financial Thriller* (United Kingdom: Wiley, 2011), 3.

28 "The Amazing Harry Markopolos," http://nymag.com/daily/intelligencer/2009/01/the_amazing_harry_markopolos.html.

29 D.T. Neal, W. Wood, and J.M. Quinn, "Habits: A repeat performance," *Current Directions in Psychological Science*, 15 (2006): 198–202.

30 Charles Duhigg, *The Power of Habit: Why We Do What We Do in Life and Business.* (New York, NY: Random House Publishing Group, 2014), 17-18.

31 https://andreiantoniu.com/moral-story-that-will-change-your-bad-habits, retrieved May 26, 2021.

32 W. Wood, L. Tam, and M. Guerrero Witt, "Changing Circumstances, Disrupting Habits," *Journal of Personality and Social Psychology*, 88 (2005): 918–33.

33 "Forget Big Change, Start With a Tiny Habit: BJ Fogg at TEDxFremont," http://tedxtalks.ted.com/video/Forget-big-change-start-with-a.

34 Hardy, *Compound Effect*, 89.

35 P. Lally, C.H.M van Jaarsveld, H.W.W Potts, and J. Wardle, "How Are Habits Formed: Modeling Habit Formation in the Real World." *European Journal of Social Psychology* 40, no. 6 (2010): 998–1009.

36 Jeremy Dean, *Making Habits, Breaking Habits: Why We Do Things, Why We Don't, and How to Make Any Change Stick* (United States: Hachette Books, 2013).

37 Dean, *Making Habits*, 149.

38 Chris Chase, "Lance Armstrong and Oprah Winfrey," *USA Today Sports*, January 17, 2013, https://www.usatoday.com/story/gameon/2013/01/17/lance-armstrong-oprah-interview-updates-live/1843235.

39 Bill George, *Discover Your True North* (Hoboken, NJ: Wiley, 2015), 52.

40 Chris Greenberg, "Lance Armstrong Confession: Cyclist Admits Doping During Oprah Interview," *Huff*post, January 18, 2013, http://www.huffington post.com/2013/01/17/lance-armstrong-confession-doping_n_2499996.html.

41 Amy Davidson Sorkin, "Lance Armstrong's Flawed Confession," *The New Yorker*, January 18, 2013, https://www.newyorker.com/news/amy-davidson/lance-armstrongs-flawed-confession.

42 "10 Leaders Who Aren't Afraid to Be Transparent," http://www.forbes.com/sites/johnhall/2012/08/27/10-leaders-who-arent-afraid-to-be-transparent.

43 https://www.moralstories.org/lion-and-his-fear, accessed May 22, 2021.

44 Will Bowen, *Happy This Year! The Secret to Getting Happy Once and for All* (United States: Brilliance Publishing, 2013).

45 "Oprah and Lance Armstrong: A Worldwide Exclusive," *Oprah's Next Chapter*, 01/17/2013.

46 Anthony Robbins, *Awaken the Giant Within* (Free Press, 1991), 19.

47 Brené Brown, *The Gifts of Imperfection* (United States: Hazelden Publishing, 2010), 125.

48 https://todpoles.com/english-kids-stories/moral-stories-stories/marbles-and-sweets.

49 Bowen, *Happy This Year*, 2013.

50 Brené Brown, *Daring Greatly: How the Courage to Be Vulnerable Transforms the Way We Live, Love, Parent, and Lead* (United Kingdom: Penguin Books Limited, 2013).

51 A.B. Brunell, M.H. Kernis, B.M. Goldman, W. Heppner, P. Davis, E.V. Cascio, and G.D. Webster, Dispositional authenticity and romantic relationship functioning. *Personality and Individual Differences*, 48 (2010): 900–05.

52 Miller McPherson, Lynn Smith-Lovin, Matthew E. Brashears, "Social Isolation in America: Changes in Core Discussion Networks over Two Decades," *American Sociological Review*, 2006, Vol. 71, http://www.asanet.org/images/press/docs/pdf/June06ASRFeature.pdf.

53 "The Flight from Conversation," http://www.nytimes.com/2012/04/22
/opinion/sunday/the-flight-from-conversation.html.

54 Jim Dornan and John C. Maxwell, *How to Influence People: Make a Difference in Your World* (United States: HarperCollins Leadership, 2013), 2.

55 Donald Miller, "Why Are You Loving," http://www.becauserelationships
matter.net/love-others.

56 Tolani Brendan Mosweu, *Freedom to Soar* (Sandy, UT: Aardvark Global Publishing, 2006), 191.

57 Dale Carnegie, *How to Win Friends and Influence People* (Portugal: Pandora's Box, 2021).

58 Kirsten Dixson and William Arruda, *Career Distinction* (United Kingdom: Wiley, 2007), 174.

59 Keith Ferrazzi, *Never Eat Alone: Expanded and Updated* (United States: Crown, 2014), 65.

60 Robert Lacey, *Monarch: The Life and Reign of Elizabeth II* (United Kingdom: Free Press, 2008), 283.

61 Jeremiah Gardner, "The Personal Brand Myth," *Medium*, Oct. 16, 2013, https://medium.com/better-humans/6d0174c3a4cf.

62 Suzanne Bates, *Discover Your CEO Brand: Secrets to Embracing and Maximizing Your Unique Value as a Leader* (Portugal: McGraw-Hill Education, 2011), 1.

63 Dixson and Arruda, *Career Distinction*, 14.

64 Seth Godin, "Needles, Haystacks, and Magnetism," *Seth's Blogs*, June 8, 2004, https://seths.blog/2004/06/needles_haystac.

65 Dixson and Arruda, *Career Distinction*, 17.

66 Karl Speak and David McNally, *Be Your Own Brand: Achieve More of What You Want by Being More of Who You Are* (United States: Berrett-Koehler Publishers, 2010), 14.

67 McNally and Speak, *Be Your Own Brand*, 1.

68 McDonald's Corporation, "Our Story," http://www.mcdonalds.com/us/en
/our_story.html.

69 Suzanne Bates, *Discover Your CEO Brand: Secrets to Embracing and Maximizing Your Unique Value as a Leader* (Portugal: McGraw-Hill Education, 2011).

70 Seth Godin, *Purple Cow: Transform Your Business by Being Remarkable* (United Kingdom: Portfolio, 2009).

71 "In U.S., Trust in Media Recovers Slightly from All-time Low," http://www.gallup.com/poll/164459/trust-media-recovers-slightly-time-low.aspx.

72 "Target Vows to Speed Anti-Fraud Technology," http://www.nytimes.com/2014/02/05/business/target-to-speed-adoption-of-european-anti-fraud-technology.html?_r=0.

73 "Americans' Trust in Government Generally Down This Year," http://www.gallup.com/poll/164663/americans-trust-government-generally-down-year.aspx.

74 "U.S. Economic Confidence at Lowest Level Since December," http://www.gallup.com/poll/167387/economic-confidence-lowest-level-december.aspx.

75 "In U.S., Political Trust in 'American People' at New Low," http://www.gallup.com/poll/164678/political-trust-american-people-new-low.aspx.

76 https://www.publishyourarticles.net/knowledge-hub/articles/a-short-moral-story-on-do-not-play-upon-the-credibility-of-others-for-kids/4773.

77 John C. Maxwell, *Put Your Dream to the Test: 10 Questions that Will Help You See It and Seize It* (United States: Thomas Nelson, 2011), 124.

78 Interview with Daniel Goleman, "Why Aren't We More Compassionate?" *NPR TED Radio Hour,* Dec. 19, 2014, https://www.wkms.org/2014-12-19/why-arent-we-more-compassionate.

79 Goleman, *NPR,* 2014.

80 https://www.goodreads.com/quotes/96302-make-no-judgments-where-you-have-no-compassion.

81 Barbara Pachter, *The Power of Positive Confrontation* (Boston, MA: Da Capo Lifelong Press, 2014).

82 Beverly Engel, *The Power of Apology: Healing Steps to Transform All Your Relationships* (Germany: Wiley, 2002).

83 "The Reincarnation of Mike Milken," http://www.businessweek.com/1999/99_19/b3628001.htm.

84 Harvey Mackay, *The Mackay MBA of Selling in the Real World* (United States: Penguin Publishing Group, 2011), 40.

85 Susan Cain, *Quiet: The Power of Introverts in a World That Can't Stop Talking* (United Kingdom: Broadway Paperbacks, 2013), 57.

86 Bob Rosen, *Grounded: How Leaders Stay Rooted in an Uncertain World* (Germany: Wiley, 2013), 9.

87 Rosen, *Grounded*, 11.

88 Brad Lomenick, *The Catalyst Leader: 8 Essentials for Becoming a Change Maker* (United States: Thomas Nelson, 2013), 126.

89 Attributed to Mother Teresa.

90 Dirk van Dierendonck and Kathleen Patterson, *Servant Leadership: Developments in Theory and Research* (United Kingdom: Palgrave Macmillan UK, 2010), x.

91 Robert K. Greenleaf, *The Power of Servant-leadership: Essays* (United States: Berrett-Koehler Publishers, 1998), 8.

92 Pat Williams, *Coaching Your Kids to Be Leaders: The Keys to Unlocking Their Potential* (United States: FaithWords, 2008).

93 Williams, *Coaching Your Kids*, 219.

94 Robert Greenleaf, *The Power of Servant-Leadership* (Berrett-Koehler Publishers, Inc., 1998), 114.

95 Henry David Thoreau, *Walden: Or, Life in the Woods.*

96 Stephen R. Covey, *First Things First* (New York, NY: Free Press, 1994), 45.

97 *The Silent Angel Documentary*, 2020.

98 Arianna Huffington, "Are You Living Your Eulogy or Your Résumé?" *Huffpost*, Sept. 23, 2013, https://www.huffpost.com/entry/are-you-living -your-eulogy-or-your-resume_b_3936937.

99 Winston Churchill, *Churchill: The Power of Words*, ed. Martin Gilbert (Boston: Da Capo Press, 2012), 25–26, Kindle. (Also see Jonathan Sandys, Wallace Henley, James Baker. *God & Churchill: How the Great Leader's Sense of Divine Destiny Changed His Troubled World and Offers Hope for Ours* (Tyndale House, 2015).

100 Brené Brown, *The Gifts of Imperfection* (United States: Hazelden Publishing, 2010), 7.

101 Brown, *Gifts*, 15.

102 Marianne Williamson, *Return to Love* (New York, NY: Harper-Collins, 1992), 190–91.

103 "How Lolo Jones Can Rebound from Poor Start in Sochi," http: //bleacherreport.com/articles/1965906-how-lolo-jones-can-rebound-from -poor-start-in-sochi#ooid=xwdjBpazrVaQ0DkuQ8hzR9QWAwEDz185.

104 Ibid.

105 Ibid.

106 Michael Reid Davis, *Discovering Your Authentic Power* (United States: Vantage Press, 2009).

107 https://www.goodreads.com/quotes/35835-strength-does-not-come-from -winning-your-struggles-develop-your.

108 https://ftw.usatoday.com/2016/02/best-sports-quotes-about-winning.

109 Megan Dalla-Camina, *Simple Soulful Sacred: A Woman's Guide to Clarity, Comfort and Coming Home to Herself* (United States: Hay House, 2019).

110 Eric Zorn, "Without Failure, Jordon Would Be False Idol," *Chicago Tribune*, May 19, 1997, https://www.chicagotribune.com/news /ct-xpm-1997-05-19-9705190096-story.html.

111 Wayne Mazzoni, *You Vs You: Sports Psychology for Life* (Northport, NY: Mazz Marketing Inc., 2005), 25.

112 Mia Hamm, *Go for the Goal: A Champion's Guide to Winning in Soccer and Life* (United States: It Books, 2013), 6.

113 Suresh Mohan Semwal, *Best Management Quotes* (New Delhi, India: Prabhat Prakashan, 2008), 82.

114 http://www.vincelombardi.com/number-one.html.

115 https://themindsjournal.com/owning-our-story-can-be-hard-but-not -nearly-as-difficult.